融媒体实验与实践工作坊

Integration Media Experiment & Practice Workshop

主编 | 金云水　徐逸君

Chief Editor | Jin Yunshui　Xu Yijun

同济大学出版社

TONGJI UNIVERSITY PRESS

目录 Contents

卷首语 Foreword

从2014年开始，我参与了工作坊课程的每一次筹备规划会议，亲眼见证着这项教学改革课程的成长。这四年，不变的是课程设计的理念——让学生获得切实的成长。秉承着这样的信念，四年工作坊，我们每一年都在课程设计上下足功夫，并根据学生的反馈不断做出调整与突破：第一年保险起见采用了套餐式课程；第二年尝试了自由度更高但组织难度颇大的“拼盘式”课程；第三年则在“拼盘式”课程的基础上规定了限选课程，避免学生只选择自己擅长的课程。每一年都为学生引进较为前沿的课程，从第一年的“三维扫描”“三维打印”到第二年的“飞手摄影”“VR短片制作”到第三年的“H5设计”“动作捕捉技术”“电竞解说”。越来越多地为学生引进业界的资源，包括东道集团设计总监、腾讯资深声音设计师、INX渲染总监等；为了让同学们可以相互熟识，第三年重新引入了“破冰活动——互动Party”；课程组织上也由最开始的邮件选课升级为手机app选课，三次分组小汇报合并升级为有节目表演、有抽奖评分的大汇报盛宴。

学生们的成长是这门课程设置的初衷。每年工作坊的学生日志我都要看至少三遍，这几百本日志记录的是每一名学生对工作坊三轮课程学习的心路历程。第一年看日志我是紧张的、是拒绝的，我很担心在大家的日志中感受到失望与抱怨。隔了好几天才鼓起勇气翻开日志，结果看了几本便停不下来，一不小心就一口气看完了全部的日志。我看到了同学们的辛苦与充实；看到了字里行间洋溢着的成就感；看到了“跨界”的融合与尝试——动画的同学开始拍片子，广告的同学玩起了手绘逐格动画（还获了奖）。更让人欣慰的是，我看到了很多同学独立思考的能力，不少同学在日志中对工作坊课程设计、组织以及细节执行献计献策，后被我们逐一采纳。课程带给了学生们成长，而学生们的反馈又悄无声息地促进了工作坊的成长。

工作坊是一年级学生开启大二生涯前的第一课，两天一轮的课程对于技能本身的提高是有限的，但是为未来做事情、做学问埋下了一颗种子。很多同学为了完成理想的作品，在实验室通宵加班制作。虽然最后完成的作品还显得粗糙与稚嫩，但熬了夜、用了心的同学收获的快乐怕是只有经历过的人才能有所体会。有些同学反过头来回忆这段高强度的学习时光，说整个大一一年都没有这么累过，现在想起来竟然觉得很怀念。这个辛苦甚至有些痛苦的过程是极好的经历，它会切实地让你明白做学问、学知识是没有捷径可走的，务必脚踏实地。工作坊是大一的收尾，也是后面三年的开始，帮助同学们树立拼搏精神，端正学习态度，为媒体与艺术行业艰辛的从业做好准备，这就是我们的“第一课”想给同学们带来的东西。

十年树木，百年树人，四岁的工作坊还有很长的路要走。我心里很清楚明年、后年、未来，工作坊要不断面临新的问题与挑战。不过我也坚信我们一定会克服挑战、解决问题，看着一届又一届的学生不断成长。此刻，实验室的灯光下，学生日志摊开在桌面上，外面的月光明亮，而我同样心满意足，对工作坊的未来充满希望。

金云水

2019年9月

Since 2014, I have participated in every single preparatory planning meeting of the workshop course from beginning to end, witnessing the development of this educational reform course. In the past four years, what remained unchanged was the concept of curriculum design, which was to motivate the effective progress of the students. In accordance with this belief, we have worked hard on curriculum design every year in the four-year workshop, and constantly made adjustments and breakthroughs according to the feedback of students. In the first year, package courses were adopted for the sake of insurance. In the second year, we tried "platter" courses, which were more liberal but quite difficult to organize. In the third year, on the basis of "platter" courses, restrictions on the selection of courses were proposed, so as to prevent students from choosing only the courses they were skilled in. We introduced more cutting-edge courses for students each year. For example, "3D scanning" and "3D printing" in the first year;"photography using drones" and "VR short film production" in the second year; "H5 design", "motion capture technology", and "gaming commentary" in the third year. More than that, we introduced industrial experts for students, including design director of the DONG DAO group, senior voice designer of Tencent, rendering director of INX, etc. For the sake of familiarizing students with each other, the "ice-breaking activity- interactive party" was reintroduced in the third year. The arrangement of the courses is also upgraded from the first email course selection to mobile app course selection. The three groups of small reports are merged and upgraded to a grand report banquet with performance and lottery score.

The development of students is the initial goal of the workshop. I read the students' journals of the workshop more than three times every year. These hundreds of journals recorded varied reasoning processes of each student after learning three rounds of courses in the workshop. The first year I was nervous and refused to read the journals because I was worried about feeling disappointed and complaining in their journals. Several days later, I plucked up the courage to open students' journals. Consequently, I browsed several books and couldn't help reading all the logs in one go. I felt not only the diligence and gratifying results of students, but also the sense of achievement between the lines. I also felt integration and attempt of "cross-border". Students who major in animation began to make films. Simultaneously, students who major in advertising created hand-painted animation grid by grid and also won the prize. What's more gratifying is that I felt the ability of many students to think independently. Many students give suggestions on the course design, organization and detailed implementation of the workshop in the journals. And then we adopt them one by one. The course enables students to grow, and students' feedback quietly promotes the growth of the workshop.

The workshop is the first attempt for Grade One students to start their careers in Grade Two. A two-day course is limited to the improvement of skills, but it is beneficial to cultivate the good attitude of doing things and learning in the future. Many students worked overtime all night in the laboratory to complete their ideal works. The final work was rough and immature. However, the joy of staying up late and harvesting after hardwork could only be experienced by those who had done their utmost. Some students looked back on this experience and indicated they had never been so tired during the year of Grade One. They cherished the time when they study very hard. This hard, even painful process is an excellent experience for them to realize that there is no shortcut to mastering any knowledge. Everyone should be steadfast in his/her work. The workshop marked the end of Grade One and the beginning of the next three years. We hope that this workshop can help students to set up a striving spirit correcting their learning attitude, and prepare themselves for the rigorousness of the media and art industry. This is what our "first lesson" wants to bring to the students.

It takes ten years to grow a tree, but a hundred to cultivate a person. The four-year-old workshop still has a long way to go. I know that the workshop will continue to face new problems and challenges in the future. But I also firmly believe that we will overcome challenges and solve problems. Ultimately, we will see the development of the students. At this moment, the student journal is placed on the desktop, and the moonlight outside is bright. I hold full expectations about the future of the workshop with deep satisfaction.

JIN Yunshui

September 2019

工作坊日志一页 17 级动画 张天鹤

The page of workshop log Zhang Tianhe, a student majoring in Animation of Grade 2017

介绍 Introduction

教学大纲

Syllabus

一、课程概述

Course Overview

同济大学艺术与传媒学院“融媒体实验与实践工作坊”，面向学院所有一年级升二年级的本科生，包括动画、广播电视编导、广播电视学、广告、音乐表演、影视表演等专业，在2017-2018学年春季学期第20～21周的连续10天内开展。课程共包含14门子课程，每个学生需自由选择3门子课程作为一组课程模块并完成学习，每门子课程持续2天。所有课程均以工作坊的形式教学，学生的最终成绩将由其选择的3门子课程成绩以及其记录的学习日志成绩共同构成。

The "Media Experimental and Practical Workshop" of College of Arts & Media of Tongji University, aimed at all freshmen, including Animation, Radio and Television Editor, Radio and Television Science, Advertising, Music Performance, and Film & Television Performance. It was held within 10 days from the 20th to 21st academic week of the spring semester of 2017-2018 academic year. There were 14 courses in the workshop. Each student was free to choose 3 courses as a group of module, and completed the learning. Each course lasted 2 days. All the courses were taught in the form of workshop. The final score of a student was composed of the results of the 3 courses he chose, and the records of his study log.

二、课程目标

Course Objective and Requirements

本课程旨在以工作坊的形式，通过跨学科、跨领域课程的引入，提高学生的动手能力、培养学生的横向拓展能力，进而综合提升他们在媒体领域的基础素养。

The purpose of this course was to improve students' practical ability and cultivate their ability to expand horizontally, by introducing interdisciplinary courses in the form of workshop, so as to comprehensively improve their basic literacy in the field of media.

三、教学内容

Lesson Topics

拼盘式子课程:

课程共包含 14 门子课程，每门子课程持续 2 天。每名学生需自由选择 3 门子课程作为一组课程模块完成学习。

Buffet-mode Course:

There were 14 courses, each lasting 2 days. Each student was free to choose 3 courses as a group of module, and completed the learning.

A 树脂立体画
B 木版水印
C 中国书法
D 版式与色彩设计
E 品牌策划与活动设计
F 展览设计快速入门到实践
G 延时摄影
H 特效摄影与高速摄影
I 网络短视频制作
J 影视作品的声音设计
K 台词对白
L 影视特效化妆
M 媒介文化
N 领略神奇的 AR 技术

A 3D Resin Painting
B Chinese Traditional Watercolor Woodblock Printing
C Chinese Calligraphy
D Format and Color Design
E Brand Scheme and Activity Design
F Exhibition Design from Quick Start to Practice
G Time-lapse Photography
H Special Effects & High-speed Photography
I The Production of Internet Videos
J Sound Design for Film and Video
K Lines & Dialogues Lesson
L Special Effects Make-up for Film and TV Works
M Media Culture
N Getting to Know AR

课程流程

Schedule

课程：

课程以实践型内容为核心，秉持“做中学”的教学理念。14 门拼盘式课程中的 3 门课程组成一个模块，每门课程的学习周期为连续 2 整天，学生需在 10 天中的 6 天完成必修的课程模块。同时，依据校内外教师的个人时间和学生的选课情况分别开设一至三轮，保证每个班级的人数都在 15 人及以下，并达到实践教学的效果。

为了提高学习效果，本期工作坊预留了一轮课程时间供学生自主选择课程旁听，并有一整天的总结时间让学生总结学习成果、完成学习日志。在最后一天的闭幕式汇报上，由教师推荐的学生汇报每门课程的优秀作业。

Courses：

With the concept of “Learning by doing”, all the lessons are practicing-centered. The buffet-mode course consists of 14 lessons, with 3 lessons as a module and each lesson lasts 2 consecutive days. All the students need to complete the required lessons as a module in 6 days of this 10-day semester. Meanwhile, each lesson will be set from 1 to 3 rounds according to teachers' personal schedule, while the students' choices are also taken into consideration. Every class has 15 students or fewer to guarantee the effectiveness of practical teaching.

The workshop of this year allows 3 days for students to finish their assignments, summarize the study achievements and complete their personal logs. The students recommended by teachers will present excellent works at the closing ceremony held on the last day of the course.

选课

Lesson Registration

2018.07.06

第一轮课程

First Round

07.16 - 07.17

第二轮课程

Second Round

07.18 - 07.19

选课规则：

14 门拼盘式课程不做组合直接面向所有学生，学生按照意愿从中自由选择 3 门课程并进行排序。在规定时间内，进行网上选课，要求如实填写姓名、手机、邮箱、学号、专业等个人信息，依次选择六个不同的课程志愿。

Rules for Registration：

14 buffet-mode lessons are open to all students without combination. Students are required to reorder 3 lessons from all the lessons according to their own preferences, with favorite lessons in the front. Students can choose lessons at the scheduled time, and personal information like their name, mobile phone number, email address, student number and major are required to be completed truthfully. They should choose 6 different lessons in turn.

录取规则：

选课录取以网上报名的时间先后、专业优先级、课程类别与课程容量为依据。根据网上报名的先后顺序，录取学生前三个志愿。若学生前三个志愿中的某一课程容量已满，则以学生志愿排序为依据，录取下一个课程容量未满的志愿，以此类推；若学生的六个志愿均达到课程容量，则以课程容量为依据，直至所有学生均录取三门课程为止。

选课结果及相应的课程表将以电子邮件的形式反馈给学生。

Rules for Enrollment：

Admission standards are based on the selection time, major priority, types of lesson and lesson capacity. Per the sequential order of online selection, the first three preferred lessons will be chosen. If one of the three preferred lessons reaches its maximum capacity, the next preferred lesson will be chosen instead. If the six preferred lessons all reach the peak point, another three lessons can be chosen to meet the requirements.

Lastly, the enrollment information and the corresponding schedule are sent to every student via email.

第三轮课程
Third Round
07.20 - 07.21

作品汇报
& 闭幕式
Presentation &
Graduation Ceremony
2018.07.21
17:00 - 20:00

总评
(课程日志)
Assessment
(log)

课程总评：

除了完成课程以外，学生还需要提交学习日志，日志内容可包括学习心得体会、课堂笔记、作业成果等。

课程成绩由 3 门课程分数及学习日志分数共同构成，各占 25%。其中课程成绩由任课教师评定，课程日志由评定小组评定。

Assessment：

Besides assignments given by teachers, students are also asked to hand in their personal logs which can be lesson notes or achievements, thoughts or impressions, drawings or paste-up, etc.

The final mark is evaluated by two aspects, containing the scores estimated from 3 lessons and the grade of their personal logs. Note that the log takes a quarter of the final score as well as each lesson. The score of lesson is assessed by the related teacher, and the personal course log is assessed by the assessment team.

教师简介

About Teachers

廖莎莎

LIAO SHASHA

北京大学数字艺术系硕士，研究领域为三维动画制作、分镜头台本设计、动画造型设计，创作的三维动画短片多次获得国内外动画比赛奖项。

She holds a Master Degree of digital art, in School of Peking University. Her research area is 3D animation production, sub lens platform design, and animation modeling design. Her 3D animation short film has won many awards in animation competitions at home and abroad.

费俞

FEI YU

上海市中级工艺美术师，廿四节气|手艺学堂——黄木版水印工艺讲师，师承苏州桃花坞木版水印传承人顾志军。主要研究现代木版水印版画。

He is an intermediate craftsman in Shanghai. He's a lecturer in yellow wood watermark technology of "24 solar terms, Craft School". He learned from Mr. Gu Zhijun, the inheritor of woodblock watermark in Taohuawu of Suzhou. He is mainly engaged in modern woodblock printing.

梅琼林

MEI QIONGLIN

传播学教授、博士生导师、博士后导师、国务院学科评议人。研究方向为传播学基本理论、传播学思想史、传播学学科史。

He is a professor of communication, doctoral supervisor, postdoctoral supervisor, and subject reviewer of the State Council. His research direction is the basic theory of communication, the history of communication thought, the history of communication discipline.

由芳

YOU FANG

设计学教授、博士生导师，同济大学艺术与传媒学院用户体验与汽车交互设计实验室负责人。

She is a professor of design and doctoral supervisor, School of Arts & Media, Tongji University. She is the head of the User Experience / Automotive Interaction Design Lab.

王建民
WANG JIANMIN

设计学教授、博士生导师，教育部高等学校动画、数字媒体专业教学指导委员会委员，主持多项国家课题，获国内外发明专利三十余项。研究方向为交互设计、可用性工程、信息架构设计、社会媒体计算。

He is a professor of design and doctoral supervisor. He is a member of the steering committee of animation and digital media major of the Ministry of Education. He presided over many national projects, and won more than 30 invention patents at home and abroad. His research fields are interaction design, usability engineering, information architecture design, and social media computing.

汪源
WANG YUAN

现任笔克展览服务有限公司创意总监，带领团队服务过北京奥运会、上海世博会、F1 上海站等大型展示项目，以及通用汽车、SONY 等 500 强企业，目前着重于互联网 + 平台 E3 的设计管理运营。

He is currently creative director of Pico Exhibition Services Limited. He has led the team to serve the Beijing Olympic Games, Shanghai World Expo, F1 Shanghai station and other large-scale exhibition projects, as well as top 500 enterprises such as General Motors and Sony. He currently focuses on the design, management and operation of the Internet + platform E3.

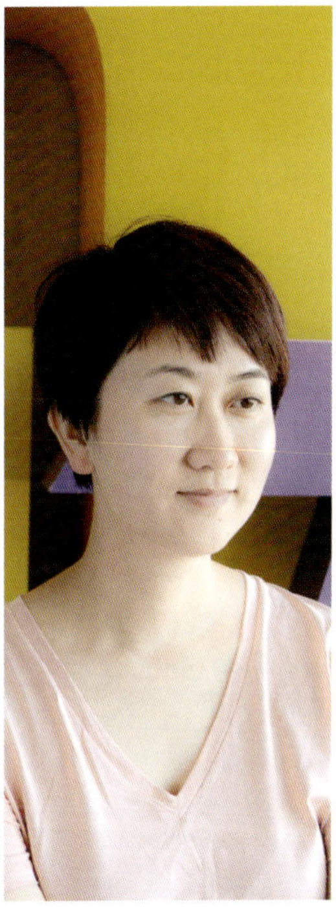

方红峰
FANG HONGFENG

北京电影学院电影美术设计创作及理论硕士。参与《乔家大院》《东归英雄传》《为爱结婚》等影视作品视觉特效制作。

She holds a Master Degree in film art design and theory from Beijing Film Academy. She has participated in the production of visual special effects in films and TV works such as *Qiao's Courtyard*, *Biography of Heroes Returning to the East*, *Marriage for Love* and so on.

薛航
XUE HANG

复旦大学物理系光学专业硕士，获教育部公派留学基金资助赴匈牙利艺术设计学院进修视觉设计，期间从事实验摄影创作。

He has a Master Degree in optics in the department of Physics, Fudan University. He went to Hungarian Institute of Art and Design for further study of visual design with the aid of the Ministry of Education's public fund for studying abroad, during which he was engaged in experimental photography creation.

任玲玲
REN LINGLING

中国传媒大学本科和硕士、同济大学博士，苹果 ACT FCP T3 国际认证讲师，上海市广播电视协会会员。研究方向为影视与新媒体。

She is a Bachelor and Master of Communication University of China, and a Doctor of Tongji University. She is an internationally certified lecturer of Apple ACT FCP T3, and a member of Shanghai Radio and Television Association. Her research direction is film & television and new media.

万方
WAN FANG

现任腾讯上海资深游戏声音设计师。毕业于浙江大学工业设计系及英国德比大学音乐技术和声音系统设计专业。主要作品有《天涯明月刀》《大话西游》等。

She is now Tencent's senior game sound designer in Shanghai. She graduated from the department of industrial design of Zhejiang University, and the major of music technology and sound system design of Derby University. Her main works are *Moonlight Blade*, *A Chinese Odyssey*, etc.

饶丹云
RAO DANYUN

资深艺术语言讲师，硕士生导师，毕业于中国传媒大学播音系，美国圣地亚哥州立大学访问学者。“中华诵”全国优秀指导老师。

She is a senior art language lecturer and master tutor. She graduated from the broadcasting department of China Media University. She is a visiting scholar at San Diego State University. She is a national excellent instructor of "Chinese recitation".

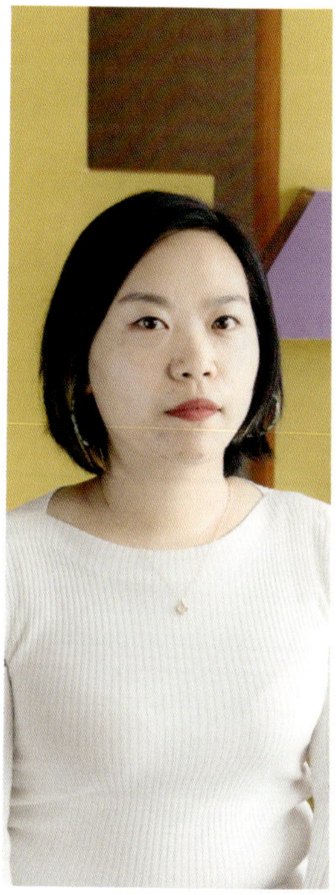

房巧玉
FANG QIAOYU

毕业于温哥华电影学院，任 "RUN FOR U LIFE" "THE LAST SIX" 《十宗罪》《鲛珠传》《妖妖铃》《三生三世之十里桃花》等院线电影、电视剧的前期翻模师、特效化妆师。

She graduated from Vancouver Film Academy. She served as the former model changer and special effects makeup artist of the cinema films and TV plays such as *RUN FOR U LIFE*, *THE LAST SIX*, *The Ten Deadly Sins*, *Legend of The Naga Pearls*, *Demon Bell*, and *Ten Great Li of Peach Blossom*.

蒋原伦
JIANG YUANLUN

博士，曾任北京师范大学文学院教授，现任同济大学高等研究院研究员，从事文艺学、文学批评、媒介批评和传播学理论方面研究。主编媒介文化研究和媒介批评丛书多种。

He is a Doctor. He used to be a professor of the School of Arts of Beijing Normal University, and now he is a researcher of the Institute of Higher Studies of Tongji University. He is engaged in the study of literature and art, literary criticism, media criticism and communication theory. He is the editor in chief of a series on media culture research and media criticism.

柳喆俊
LIU ZHEJUN

设计学副教授，曾在育碧游戏任职，有丰富的教学与创作经验。为汇丰银行、飞利浦等诸多著名品牌创作过三维动画与交互装置，作品多次获得全国大奖以及上海市讲课比赛大奖。研究方向：三维动画与后期合成、虚拟现实与交互媒体、游戏设计。

He's an associate professor of design. He used to work for Ubisoft. He has rich experience in teaching and creation. He has created 3D animation and interactive devices for many famous brands such as HSBC and Philips. His works have won many national awards, and he has won Shanghai lecture competition award. His research direction is 3D animation and post synthesis, virtual reality and interactive media, and game design.

课程简介

Course Information

树脂立体画

本课程主要讲解树脂立体画的工艺流程和制作方法，让学生通过动手实践，制作独具一格的树脂立体画，并在过程中培养细致的观察力和创造力，感受手工创作的乐趣。

安排

- 挑选容器并灌注第一层胶
- 了解工艺流程和原理，在纸上设计
- 调制、灌注与绘制

木版水印

本课程主要讲解木版水印（中国古代印刷技法）和实际操作。

安排

- 木版水印基本概况
- 雕版制作
- 印刷试色、修版

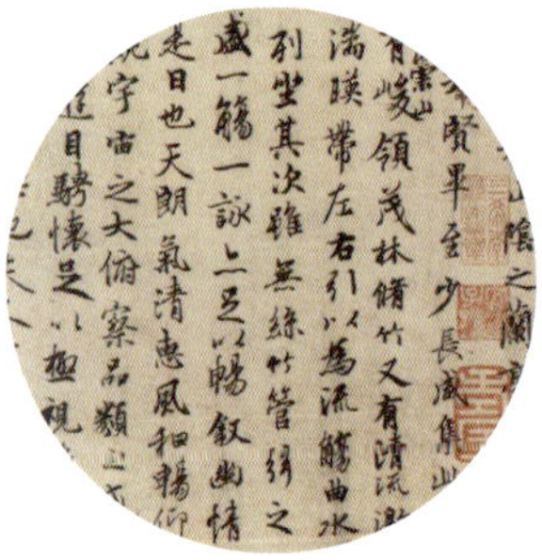

中国书法

本课程重点在观赏、书写和简要的线索勾勒实践，意在培养学生的中国书法的审美趣味及动手能力，书法的学术研究方面融入指导过程中。

安排

- 比较艺术视野中的中国书法
- 中国书法与现代东西方艺术
- 字体临摹

版式与色彩设计

本课程主要讲解基本的栅格化版式与色彩设计原理，并通过一定的教学物理模具进行现场实践和讲解。

安排

- 栅格化版式设计
- 概念和案例分析
- 色彩设计

3D Resin Painting

This course introduces the technological process and production method of 3D resin painting. It helps students make unique 3D resin painting through hands-on practice activities. And in this process, students are able to cultivate meticulous observation and creativity, and feel the fun of hand-made creation.

Keynote

- Select the container and pour the first layer of glue
- Understand process flow and principle, design on paper
- Modulate, pour into and draw

Chinese Traditional Watercolor Woodblock Printing

This course mainly introduces Chinese traditional watercolor woodblock printing (ancient Chinese printing techniques) and practical operation.

Keynote

- Basic overview of Chinese traditional watercolor woodblock printing
- Engraving production
- Printing color test and plate repair

Chinese Calligraphy

This course focuses on viewing, writing and sketching. This course aims to cultivate students' aesthetic taste and practical ability of Chinese calligraphy. The academic research of calligraphy is integrated into the guidance process.

Keynote

- Chinese calligraphy from the perspective of comparative art
- Chinese calligraphy and the trend of modern eastern and western art
- Theory of Chinese calligraphy font copy

Format and Color Design

This course mainly introduces the basic principles of grid layout and color design. On-site practice and explanation is carried out through a certain teaching physical tools.

Keynote

- Grid layout design
- Concept and case analysis
- Color design

品牌策划与活动设计

本课程围绕智能网联汽车产业发展的趋势，通过组织学生集体讨论、邀请汽车领域传媒企业客串等方式展开相关竞赛品牌和竞赛内容的设计。

安排

- 智能化汽车产业背景概述
- 品牌策划内容设计创意
- 智能汽车竞赛活动策划

展览设计快速入门到实践

本课程主要让学生对展览设计有个快速全面的认识，了解展览设计中特别需要注意的关键点，包括如何读懂客户需求、如何看懂平面图、如何实际设计一个完整展台、认识展览常用材质、了解施工工艺以及最后落地执行的过程，快速成为展览设计师。

安排

- 展览设计基础理论
- 展览设计实际应用技巧
- 案例实际操作
- 案例设计

延时摄影

本课程主要讲解延时摄影的设备、拍摄条件、现场拍摄、后期制作。

安排

- 延时摄影案例分析
- 延时摄影的设备和拍摄条件
- 延时摄影实践
- 后期制作

Brand Scheme and Activity Design

The course focuses on the development trend of Intelligent Connected Vehicle. Students are invited to participate in group discussion. Media enterprises in the automobile industry are invited to participate in the design of relevant competition brands and competition contents.

Keynote

- An overview of the background of intelligent automobile industry
- Design creativity of brand planning content
- Planning on smart car competition

Exhibition Design from Quick Start to Practice

This course aims to give students a quick and comprehensive understanding of exhibition design. It enables students to understand the key points in exhibition design, including how to understand customers' needs, how to understand the planar graph, and how to actually design a complete booth. It enables students to know the materials commonly used in the exhibition, understand the construction process and the final landing process, and quickly become exhibition designers.

Keynote

- Basic theory of exhibition design
- Practical application skills of exhibition design
- Case practice
- Case design

Time-lapse Photography

This course mainly introduces the equipment, shooting conditions, on-site shooting and post production of time-lapse photography.

Keynote

- Case analysis of time-lapse photography
- Equipment and shooting conditions of time-lapse photography
- Practice of time-lapse photography
- Post production

特效摄影与高速摄影

本课程主要讲解在创意广告摄影中常见的一些特效拍摄技巧，并结合一定的视频高速摄影技术，指导学生在最短时间内获得专业工作室摄影的实践体验。

安排

- 特效摄影器材与高速摄影技术介绍
- 火焰特效高速摄影拍摄
- 水花运动特效及高速拍摄

网络短视频制作

本课程主要讲解近两年网络短视频的特点和创意，结合视听表达技巧，制作具有知识性和趣味性的短视频。

安排

- 网络短视频概述
- 视频制作基础
- 视频制作

影视作品的声音设计

本课程主要讲解声音设计在影视作品中的重要性，以及如何根据不同的影视场景进行声音素材的设计、制作和剪辑成品。

安排

- 声音设计的基本概念
- 影视片段的挑选及声音设计
- 影视声音的制作流程
- 制作影视片段的声音成品

Special Effects & High-speed Photography

This course mainly introduces some common special effects shooting skills in creative advertising photography, and combines some video high-speed photography technology. This course guides students to gain practical experience of professional studio photography in the shortest time.

Keynote

- Introduction of special effects photographic equipment and high-speed photography technology
- High-speed photography of flame effect
- Special effects and high-speed shooting of spray movement

The Production of Internet Videos

This course mainly introduces the characteristics and creativity of short online video in the past two years. Combined with audio-visual expression skills, short videos with knowledge and interest are produced.

Keynote

- Overview of network short video
- The basis of video production
- Video production

Sound Design for Film and Video

This course mainly explains the importance of sound design in film and television works, and how to design, produce and edit sound materials according to different film and television scenes.

Keynote

- Basic concept of sound design
- The selection of film and television clips and sound design
- Production process of movie sound
- Production of sound products of film and television clips

台词对白

本课程以片段排演形式，进行台词对白的艺术处理技巧初步入门。每个同学必须参与一个剧目片段的排演和训练，并观摩其他片段的排演。

安排

- 报剧目，找搭档
- 台词对白技巧
- 台词表演抠戏

影视特效化妆

本课程主要讲解影视化妆造型在影视中的重要性，及让学生掌握基础制作方法、完成基础的妆面、感受影视化妆的乐趣。

安排

- 影视化妆造型的介绍及应用
- 化妆示范
- 特效化妆实践

媒介文化

本课程主旨是提高学生在媒介文化方面的研究和写作能力。

安排

- 媒介文化的由来和发展
- 媒介文化研究名著导读
- 媒介文化现象分析
- 课堂写作

领略神奇的 AR 技术

本课程通过两天时间的学习，使学生掌握进行 AR 作品创作的基本方法，创作一款有趣的 AR 作品。

安排

- VR、AR、MR 的概念及作品赏析
- 利用三维扫描技术完成三维建模
- 制作 AR 作品

Lines & Dialogues Lesson

The course is the preliminary introduction to the art processing skills of lines & dialogues in the form of segment rehearsal. Each student must participate in the rehearsal and training of a play segment, and observe the rehearsal of other segments.

Keynote

- Sign up for play, and find partners
- Skills of line dialogue
- Line performance

Special Effects Make-up for Film and TV Works

This course introduces the importance of film and television make-up modeling in film and television. It allows students to master the basic production methods, complete the basic makeup, and experience the fun of film and television make-up.

Keynote

- Introduction and application of film and television make-up modeling
- Make-up demonstration
- Practice of special effects make-up

Media Culture

The course aims to improve students' research and writing ability in media culture.

Keynote

- The origin and development of media culture
- Introduction to famous works of media culture research
- Analysis of media culture phenomenon
- Classroom writing

Getting to Know AR

The two-day course helps students master the basic methods of AR work creation and create a piece of interesting AR work.

Keynote

- Concept and works appreciation of VR, AR and MR
- Using 3D scanning technology to complete 3D modeling Import 3D model into engine design
- Make AR works

工作坊日志一页 17 级动画 林芷萱

The page of workshop log Lin Zhixuan, a student majoring in Animation of Grade 2017

问道 Q&A

树脂立体画

3D Resin Painting

Q：为什么选择树脂立体画作为教学主要内容？

A：我最近一年都在接触树脂立体画，自己也做了不少作品。我觉得树脂立体画很有意思，很容易出效果。对于学生来说，他们不需要有多么深的绘画功底，同样能做出不错的作品。我觉得树脂立体画比较适合应用在一些短小的课程中，做类似于一个小项目一样的东西。此外，我喜欢每次工作坊都更换教学内容，因而这次选择了树脂立体画。

Q: Why do you choose 3D resin painting as the main teaching content?

A: I have been exposed to 3D resin painting since last year, and I have done a lot of works myself. I think that 3D resin painting is very interesting and effective. For students, they don't need a great knowledge of painting to make good works. I think 3D resin painting is more suitable for some short courses, doing something similar to a small project. In addition, I like to change the teaching content in every workshop, so I choose 3D resin painting this time.

Q：在这门课中，您觉得对于学生来说，哪些内容是难点？

A：同学们应该会遇到两大难点。一是不知该如何分层：他们知道自己想画的内容，但是不知道怎样才能像切片一样把它分成四个层次，分别画在四层东西上。一般学生都会跟我讨论，我会帮他们分析哪一个部分画在哪一层。二是胶干得比较慢：以前都是等 24 小时胶才干，这次由于课程时间限制，我使用了加热垫，大约 10 个小时就能干。但是如果学生画得比较慢，画到中午才结束，晚上胶还干不了，就只能在教室苦等。总体来说，这门课程不算太难，只是等待时间较长。

Q: In this course, what do you think are the difficulties for students?

A: Students may encounter two major difficulties. One is that they don't know how to stratify. They know what they want to paint, but they don't know how to divide it into four layers like slices, and paint on four different layers. Generally, students discuss with me, and I help them analyze which part of the painting is on which layer. The other is that the glue dries slowly. Previously I had to wait 24 hours for glue to dry. This time, due to limitation of the course time, I used the heating pad. And the glue could be dry in about 10 hours. But if the students draw slowly and finish it at noon, the glue cannot be dry in evening, and they have to wait in the classroom. Generally speaking, this course is not too difficult, but it takes a long time to wait.

木版水印

Chinese Traditional Watercolor Woodblock Printing

Q：您可以谈谈学习版画的过程对于学生的意义吗？

A：学生会了解版画，知道我们中国的版画技法也是很高明的。这次制作的版画底本选择了几幅浮世绘作品，但是制作的手法是中国的。对色彩制作步骤作了浓缩简化，这样通过两天的课程学生就可以完成一幅完整的作品。

日本的版画技术是由中国传入的，中国明清的外来文化给日本美术带去了全新的影响。浮世绘的制作手法与中国传统版画相似，都是用木版雕刻。我想通过课程让学生了解其与中国传统版画之间的渊源，了解中国传统版画对浮世绘乃至日本文化产生的重要影响，不只是技法上，同时是精神层面的影响。

通过制作版画，也希望能够激发学生对传统手工艺的保护与传承之心。

Q: Can you talk about the significance of the process of learning printmaking for students?

A: Students will learn about printmaking, and come to realize that our Chinese printmaking techniques are also very good. The printmaking base is selected from several Ukiyo paintings, but the method of production is Chinese. The process of color production is condensed and simplified so that students can finish a complete work through a two-day course.

Japanese printmaking technology was introduced from China, and the culture of Ming and Qing Dynasties brought a new influence to Japanese art. Ukiyo painting is similar to traditional Chinese printmaking, and they are all carved with woodcut. I want students to understand the origin between Japanese printmaking and Chinese traditional printmaking, and understand the important influence of Chinese traditional printmaking on Ukiyo painting and even Japanese culture. The influence is not only in techniques, but also in spiritual level.

By printmaking, I also hope to inspire students to protect and inherit traditional crafts.

中国书法
Chinese Calligraphy

Q：您是怎么想到将中国书法作为课程主题？

A：书法是中国的国粹啊，具体说应该是国粹中的国粹，也是校园文化不可或缺的一部分。像同济大学校徽上的题字堪称经典，号称“七分半书”，即楷、行、草、隶、篆各取一分，颜柳各取一分，何绍基取半分。字形飘洒圆秀、弯弓盘马、沉雄峭拔，恣肆中见逸气，忽似壮士如牛，筋骨涌现，堪称“师古而不泥古，尊法而求新变”。

书法绝对不是小事，不是文化之外的小技巧。它在我们的学术素养中是一个极重要的环节。在多年的教学过程中，我真切地感受到了中国书法字体变化中体现的历史感，书法真迹中的每一个字、每一个细节都值得我们去珍视、欣赏。

Q: Why do you regard Chinese calligraphy as the theme of the course?

A: Calligraphy is the quintessence of China. Specifically, it should be the quintessence of Chinese quintessence. It is also an indispensable part of campus culture. For example, the inscription on the emblem of Tongji University, it can be called "Seven-and-a-half-script". Namely, regular script, running script, cursive script, official script and seal script each takes one point, Yan and Liu each takes one point, Shaoji He takes half point. Characters float round and elegant, bow and horse bend, steep and elevated, and free spirit is seen in wanton, like heroes as cattle, bones and tendons emerge, which can be called "learning from the past but not sticking to the past, respecting the law and seeking new changes".

Calligraphy is absolutely not a trivial matter, not a trivial skill outside of culture. It is a very important link in our academic literacy. Through many years of course-teaching, I really feel the historical sense reflected in the change of Chinese calligraphy fonts. Each word and detail in the authentic work of Chinese calligraphy, is worth cherishing and appreciating.

版式与色彩设计
Format and Color Design

Q：老师您为什么要开设“版式与色彩设计”这门课？

A：我觉得这门课程很有意义，可以通过两天的学习充分锻炼学生的动手能力，让他们体验一些与众不同的东西。对于我来说，这也是另外一种教学方式的尝试。过程中，我会让学生先了解一定的原理和思路，在他们有了理性的思维之后，再有目的地让他们动手。

Q: Why do you want to offer the course “Format and Color Design”?

A: I think this course is very meaningful. Through two-day study, students can fully exercise their hands-on ability, so that they can experience something different. For me, this is another way of teaching. In the process, I will let students first understand certain principles and ideas. After they have rational thinking, I will purposefully let them operate.

Q：您在这门课中用到了一些色块，这有哪些特殊的作用？

A：这门课的主要目的就是通过造型、布局、色彩去表达一种情感或者认知。相较于人眼可以关注到的色彩或者布局，我更希望同学们能够描述除了视觉以外的，类似于轻、重、速度感、活跃、平和等人体的感受，通过色块等形式进行情感的表达和认知的改变。

Q: You have used some color blocks in this course. What special functions do they have?

A: The main purpose of this course is to express an emotion or cognition through shape, layout and color. Compared with the color or layout that people can pay attention to, I hope that students can describe the feelings of human body besides vision, such as light, heavy, sense of speed, active and peaceful. The emotional expression and cognitive change are carried out in the form of color blocks.

品牌策划与活动设计
Brand Scheme and Activity Design

Q：您为什么想要开设这门课程？

A：一方面同济大学汽车专业本身比较强，经常参与国家重点研发计划；另一方面现在国内各大学都开始组织一些以汽车为主题的学生活动。赛车活动一是具有科技性，二是比较年轻化、有激情，在全世界范围内也能够融合一些媒体和广告。我想借助这个题目将我们所有的专业带动起来，参与策划，这也和我们创办暑期工作坊的期望相吻合。

Q: Why do you want to offer this course?

A: On one hand, automobile major of Tongji University itself is relatively superior, and it often participates in the national key R&D plan. On the other hand, domestic universities have begun to organize some students' activities with automobile as the theme. Car racing is technological, younger and more passionate. It can also integrate some media and advertisements all over the world. I want to use this topic to motivate all our specialties, and make all our specialties participate in the planning, which is also in line with our expectations of establishing summer workshops.

Q：学生对课程的反馈如何？您对这门课程未来的发展有什么想法？

A：反馈是两方面的。学生始终表现出浓厚的兴趣，并能够积极参与；此外我请了嘉定这边的汽车媒体企业人士来给学生做指导，他从学生的作品里看到了一些亮点，所以愿意在下学期为我们整个课程内容做主题支持，让我们的学生来做实践。这也可以算作工作坊课程的一个副产品。通过工作坊展现了我们学生能做的事情，让外部企业、传播领域看到，让他们愿意资助下学期的活动策划，这样学生可以有机会参与比较高端的品牌活动。

Q: What are the students' feedback on the course? What do you think about the future development of this course?

A: Feedback is twofold. Students always show strong interest, and can actively participate in it. In addition, I invited an expert of automobile media enterprise in Jiading to give guidance to the students. He found some bright spots in the students' works, so he is willing to do the theme support for the whole course content next semester, and let our students do the practice. This can also be regarded as a by-product of workshop courses. Through the workshop, we show what our students can do. Both enterprises and the field of communication can see what our students can do, and they may be willing to subsidize the event planning of next semester. This way students can have the opportunity to participate in more high-end brand activities.

展览设计快速入门到实践

Exhibition Design from Quick Start to Practice

Q: 您是如何安排这两天的课程的，从入门到实践？

A: 入门是讲一些比较基础的概念。我发现有些学生，一旦掌握了入门的知识以后，他就会有强烈的意愿想要早一点步入社会，早一点看到有一份收入可以实现自己的经济价值。所以我觉得对于他们来说，这门课程应该是能够满足一定需求的，因为展览设计入门相对简单，而之后实践方面就可以给他们一些好的正在发生的案例。他们应该知道什么样的设计才是好的，是可以在展览上展示的作品。

Q: 您在课程中注重培养学生哪一块的能力？

A: 我会比较注重培养他们创作故事的能力。我希望他们现在就可以明白，一个好的设计师必须要有故事，不是单纯从造型上好看或者颜色上好看这方面去做，而是有深度的一个设计。我跟他们举例，之前一个动画专业的学长作品“Harry”为什么能够拿奖，它的设计水平其实是很正常的发挥，但是它的故事、对人心灵的触动，是别人没办法比的，升华到了一定程度。所以任何的设计都是一定要有升华的。

Q: How do you arrange the two-day courses, from introduction to practice?

A: The introduction is about some basic concepts. I find some students will have strong desire to enter the society earlier, and own the income to realize their economic value earlier, once they have acquired the knowledge of entry. So I think for them, this course should be able to meet certain demands. Because the introduction of exhibition design is relatively simple, and then practice can give them some good ongoing cases. They should know what kind of design is good, and can be displayed in the exhibition.

Q: What kind of ability do you focus on fostering students during the course?

A: I focus on developing their ability to create stories. I hope they understand now a good designer must have a story. It's not just a design that looks good in shape or color, but a design with depth. I give them an example. Why “Harry”, the work of a former student majoring in animation, can win the prize? Its design level is very normal in fact. But its stories which touch on people's hearts are beyond comparison with others, and have been sublimated to a certain extent. So there must be sublimation in any design.

延时摄影

Time-Lapse Photography

Q：第二次开设这门课程，相较上学期有什么不同？

A：这个学期有一个新要求，就是要大家在创作的时候，不仅仅是实现技术，而是要把自己的想法做一个结构，每两个同学一个组，作业里面是有其精神内涵或者说主题的。相较于去年只是去实践这个技术手段，更加注重大家内心想要表达的东西。

Q: It' the second time for you to offer the course. What's the difference between this and the last one?

A: There is a new request this semester. When they create, they should not only employ technology, but also make a structure of their own ideas. Every two students are in a group. There is spiritual connotation or theme in the works. Compared with only practicing the technological means last year, I pay more attention to what students want to express in their hearts.

Q: How to balance technology and content in time-lapse photography?

A: Technology is always the foundation, and it's a means. It's amazing when you don't master it. But it's acquired knowledge, just like what you learned from childhood to college. It should be slowly transformed into empirical knowledge. When we do empirical creation, we add our subjective consciousness and form expression into it. Of course, this is definitely a step up from pure technology.

Q：在延时摄影中技术与内容如何保持平衡？

A：技术永远是基础，这是一种手段。当你没有掌握这个手段的时候你会觉得它很神奇，但这只是一个习得性的知识，就和从小到大学习的那些知识是一样的。要慢慢把它往经验知识上去靠。在经验创作的时候，我们会把自己的主观意识和形态表达加入进去，当然这肯定比纯粹的技术要提升一个档次。

特效摄影与高速摄影
Special Effects & High-speed Photography

Q：老师您开这门课的初衷是什么？

A：开这门课实际上还是配合实验中心当时的教学改革，对于暑期实践的教学改革。具体到这门课的内容设计上，我主要是考虑怎么能够在最短的时间里面，把摄影中最精要的部分体现出来。

专业摄影最重要的内容主要有两点：第一点，要想创作出有水准的作品，它的知识范畴必然会比较广，不能只限于摄影器材、技术方面，而是要有关于你的拍摄对象、你的拍摄主题、你的拍摄背景的很多知识，等到这些都全面了，才有可能拍摄出有感染力的、有水准的作品。这是摄影这个专业的特点当中，第一个需要我们认识到的。

第二点，静态图片摄影的表现力核心，就在于对一个事件，或者说是一个运动的对象，它的运动变化或者说发展最关键的一个瞬间，又或者说是最有价值的一个瞬间，对这样的一个瞬间进行清晰的、准确的画面表现。这是摄影在创作表现上的一个重要的技巧或者说是方法。

所以我希望通过两天的课程，学生能够体会到这两点的重要性。这两点都是普适性的、原则性的，是对于摄影这个广泛的领域而言的，并不局限于某一类的摄影。我希望同学们通过一个小范围的短期学习，能够领会到大范围的长期的一些价值、意义，或者说是一些观念。

Q: What is your original intention to offer the course?

A: In fact offering the course is in line with the teaching reform of the experimental center, and the reform about summer practice. Specifically to the content design of this course, I mainly consider how to reflect the most essential part of photography in the shortest time.

There are two main points in professional photography. Firstly, if you want to create a high-quality work, the scope of knowledge must be wider. Besides photographic equipment and technology, you need to have a lot of knowledge about your target, your subject and your background. Only when all of these mentioned above are complete can it be possible to produce an infectious and high-level work. This is the first one we need to recognize of the characteristics of photography.

Secondly, the core of the expressive power of static photography, lies in the clear and accurate picture representation of the most critical moment of the movement change or development, or the most valuable moment, which is of an event, or a moving object. This is an important technique or method of photographic creation in creative expression.

So I hope that through the two-day course, students can realize the importance of the two points. The points are both universal and principled. It is for photography, which is a wide range of area. Namely, it is not limited to a certain kind of photography. I hope that through a small range of short-term learning, students can understand some long-term value, meaning, or ideas of a large range.

Q：学生在拍摄过程中有没有遇到比较难以实现或达成的地方？

A：有的。尤其是像下半场关于水的特效的拍摄。往往水的特效是要配合一些其他物体的，这其中的配合就是难点，因为可能需要两三个人，这两三个人往往也并不熟练，很多操作以前也没有遇到过，一上来很难达到默契的、精准的配合。另外就是对于实验物体的把握，也会存在一些问题。比如投苹果，怎样才能够准确地把苹果投到相应的位置上？力度、方向，包括每次用的苹果的大小，都会对结果产生影响。这很难把控，尤其对于文科生。我们今年操作的难度其实更大。因为金鱼是有姿态的，它不像苹果，是一个死的东西，所以更难把控，很难出现好的拍摄效果。需要控制它出现一个理想的姿态、又出现在一个理想的位置，这种各个方面都理想的状态是很难聚合在一起的。

Q: Do the students encounter difficulties in realizing or achieving during the shooting process?

A: Yes. Especially the special effects on water shooting in the second half. The special effect of water is often to cooperate with some other objects, which is no easy task. Because it may require two or three people, who are often not skilled. Many operations haven't been done before. And it is very difficult to achieve tacit and accurate cooperation at the beginning. In addition, there are also some problems in the grasp of experimental objects. For example, how can you put an apple in the corresponding position? Strength, direction, and the size of each apple used, have an impact on the results. It's very difficult to control, especially for students of liberal arts. It's more difficult for us to operate this year. Because a goldfish has posture. It's not like an apple, which is a static thing. So it's harder to control, and it's very difficult to get good shooting results. It needs to be controlled that it assumes an ideal posture and appears in an ideal position. It's very difficult that all aspects of ideal state get together.

网络短视频制作

The Production of Internet Videos

Q：您觉得在这门课上，学生应当注意的要点是什么？

A：短视频很多，两天时间又比较短，所以在制作过程中需要一个聚焦。我会给他们几个案例，让同学模仿，甚至允许他们借用其中的内容，进行二次创作。从视频制作的角度来说，时间与质量肯定是相关的，你花的时间越长，做的视频就会越好，这的确是一种应有的态度。但是我希望同学在做作业的时候，把习惯变一下，就是说大家不要加班加点。既然给你两天时间，那你就要在这两天之内把视频尽可能做得最好。所以就需要我们去调整自己的方案。有些想法可能很美好，但是要耗费很大的精力去实现，那就应该把它改变一下。

Q: What do you think students should pay attention to in this course?

A: There are many short videos, and the two-day period is relatively short. So a focus is needed in the production process. I gave students a few cases for them to imitate. And I even allowed them to borrow the contents for a second creation. From the point of view of video production, time and quality must be related. The more time you spend, the better videos you make. It's indeed a proper attitude. But I hope that when students do their homework, they change their habits. That is, they should not work overtime. Since you've given two days, you have to make the video as good as you can in the two days. We need to adjust our plan. Some ideas may be good, but they need to take a lot of energy to realize them. So they should be changed.

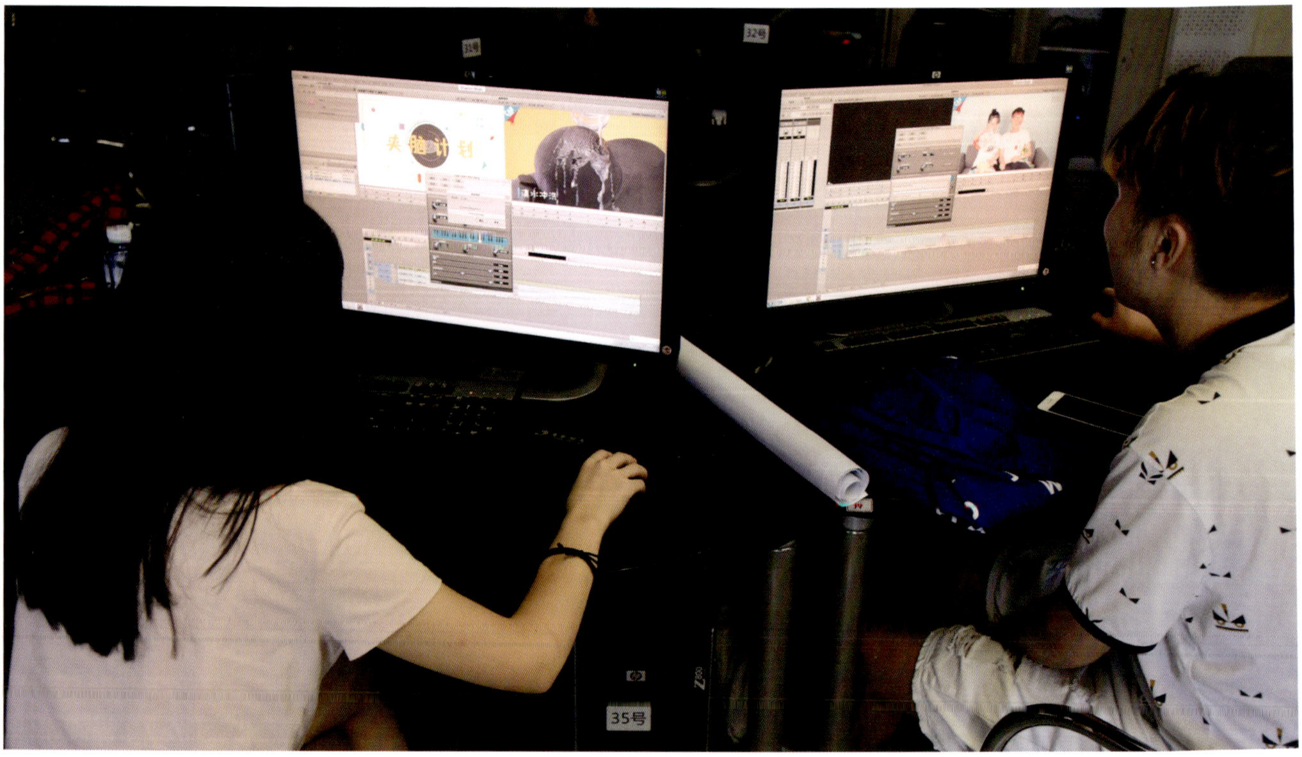

Q：老师您觉得这门课程的开展对学生的意义是什么？

A：这两年网络短视频行业处于一个爆发期，作品量很多，但是大家会发现内容层面上，其实是良莠不齐的。国家的一些监管措施，也是针对于这样一种门槛很低、所有的人都可以成为内容提供商的媒介平台。一些毫无营养和意义的作品，不论从时间还是精力上来说，对大家都是一种浪费。

短视频主要面对的人群是学生，是青年人，那么我们的同学完全可以成为优秀内容的生产商。我觉得同学们可以用一些专业的生产方式，制作出一种知识、表现出一种能力，在内容提供方面成为一股清流，或者说产生出有向上能量的内容。而且在将来，至少应该从我们自身做起，去杜绝低俗化生产。所以我觉得这门课的开展也是具有现实意义的。

Q: What do you think is the significance of this course for students?

A: In the past two years, the industry of network short videos is in an explosive period, with a large number of works. But you can find that on the content level, in fact it is uneven, namely, some good and some bad. Some national regulatory measures also aim at the media platform with low threshold, in which everyone can become content providers. Some works without nutrition and meaningfulness are a waste for all of us, whether in terms of time or energy.

Short videos mainly aim at students and young people, so our students can become producers of excellent contents. I think students can use some professional production methods to produce a kind of knowledge, show a kind of ability, become a clear stream in the content provision, or produce content with upward energy. And in the future, at least we should start by ourselves to eliminate vulgar production. So I think the development of this course is also of practical significance.

影视作品的声音设计

Sound Design for Film and Video

Q：您对学生学习的预期是？

A：因为他们都是大一升大二的学生，这方面的技术应该是几乎为零的。我希望他们通过这个课程能够对电影的声音设计有基本的了解，以后在实践中能够自己独立地完成声音的制作和后期。

Q：课程中用到的作品片段是学生根据自己的兴趣选择吗？

A：是我给他们挑了三段去掉声音的影视片段，只给他们提供声音的素材，让他们凭借这些素材把声音加到影片里面去，最后做出成品。选定片段、设计声音，其实就是想给学生一个锻炼的机会，让他们自己挑选便失去意义了。制作完成会有演示环节，每个同学上台播放自己的作品，然后做点评。

Q: What are your expectations of students' learning?

A: Because they are all freshmen, they have no knowledge in this field . I hope they can have a basic understanding of the sound design of movies during this course, and they can complete the sound production and later stage in future practice on their own.

Q: Are the pieces of work used in the course chosen by students according to their interests?

A: I picked out three clips of movies and TV, in which the sound was removed. I only provided them with sound materials, so that they could use these materials to add sound to the film, and finally made the final product. Choosing clips and designing sounds is actually to give students a chance to exercise. It makes no sense for students to choose for themselves. When the production is completed, there is a demonstration link. Each student plays his or her own work on the stage, and then comment is made.

Q：您觉得这门课程对学生发展有怎样的意义？您对课程未来有什么建议吗？

A：长远的意义，我不敢讲，因为一年只有两节课，给同学带来的东西其实是很有限的。其实之前我反映过，希望给这门课程安排的时间长一点，那我可能就有机会。比如说在学生拍片的时候去指导一下，因为对于传媒学院的学生来说，可能前期的拍片是比较重要的。如果有一个完整的流程对学生来说可能帮助更大，两天的时间，只能讲到前期、中期，后期只能给同学们点到为止吧。

Q: What do you think is the significance of this course for students' development? Do you have any suggestions for the future of the course?

A: I dare not say anything about long-term significance. Because there are only two classes in a year, what we bring to our students is actually very limited. In fact, I've asked for more time for this course. If given more time, I might have a chance, for example, to instruct students when they shoot films. Because for the students of Media College, it may be more important to shoot in the early stage. If there is a complete process, it may be more helpful for students. For two days, we can only talk about the prophase and the metaphase. For the anaphase, we can only go through the motions to the students.

台词对白

Lines & Dialogues Lesson

Q：老师您开这门课程的初衷是什么？

A：我希望把我们表演专业的课程拿出来跟其他专业的同学分享。另外，因为我知道我们学院编导专业、动画专业，包括部分新闻专业的学生，将来有一部分可能会成为剧情片或者电视文艺的导演。那么对于这部分同学来说，他们需要接触更多跟表演有关的课程，为将来的职业生涯打基础。动画专业的同学也是，他们对于人设、对于人物之间的语言，需要有一定的体验。当他有过一个真切的体验之后，具体去创作，无论是剧情片还是动画片，他在人设上、在人物的语言设置上，都会把握得更加准确。

Q: What is your original intention for this course?

A: I would like to share our acting courses with other majors. In addition, because I know that some of our college's students, majoring in director, animation, and journalism, may be directors of drama or television literature & art in the future. So for these students, they need to contact more performance-related courses to lay the foundation for their future career. For students who major in animation, they are also required to have a certain experience about both character setting and language between characters. After he has had a real experience, he will have a more accurate grasp of the setting of people and the language of characters, no matter what is a feature film or a cartoon.

Q：这几天下来，学生在表演方面有碰到困难吗？

A：因为时间非常短，表演是需要慢慢打磨的。我和同学们说，表演是一门古老的手艺，是对你自身作为动物性、作为一个人的开发。同学们主要会遇到两方面的困难，一方面是因我们的基础教育，在我们中国，中小学的基础教育里面是缺乏戏剧教育这个环节的，绝大部分学校都没有开戏剧课，学生的这种体验非常少。另一方面来自我们的学生，特别是中国的学生——现在我希望能够有所改变，我们对于肢体的东西、对于自然的东西、对于生活的东西，距离是越来越远了。离手机特别近。作为社会人的属性多，作为自然人的属性少，在课堂上的反映就是不能够大声去说话，不能够正常地走路，不能够自如地表达喜怒哀乐。并不是同学没有演技，而是我们这方面的能力真的是被封闭了。所以这是同学们面临的一个困难。再加上时间非常短，根本没有时间预热，需要学生立即投入进去。但是还好，我其实还是挺满意的，同学们的表现出乎我的意料。

Q: In the past few days, do students have any difficulties in performing?

A: The course is very short while the performance needs to be polished slowly. I tell my students that acting is an ancient craft, and it is the development of you as an animal and a person. Students encounter two main difficulties. On one hand, it's because of our basic education. In China, there is a lack of drama education in elementary and secondary education. There aren't drama lessons in most schools, and students have very little experience. On the other hand, it comes from our students, especially those in China. Now I hope to make some changes. We are farther and farther away from things of body, things of nature, and things of life. We are very close to mobile phones. There are many attributes as a social person, but few as a natural person. The reflection in class is that we can't speak loudly, walk normally and express our joys and sorrows freely. It's not that the students don't have acting skills, but our abilities in this field are really closed. So this is a difficulty that the students face. In addition, the time is very short, There is no time to warm up. And students need to be involved immediately. But fortunately, I am quite satisfied with the students' performance, which is beyond my expectation.

影视特效化妆

Special Effects Make-up for Film and TV Works

Q：学生这两天的作品中，有没有让您觉得比较惊讶、出乎意料的地方？

A：有的，虽然大多数学生零基础，从来没有接触过这个行业，但是有的作品出来，还是让我很惊讶，零基础就可以画到这种程度，比如某些用色等。有几个学生是真正领悟的，他们课下也会来问，哪里可以做到更好。其实只看作品就可以了解他是否理解这门课，哪怕只是短短的一两个小时。

Q: Is there anything, which surprises you and exceeds your expectation, in students' works?

A: Yes, there is. Although most students have no foundation and have never been in touch with this industry, I am still surprised by some of their works. The students with zero base can draw to this extent, such as some colors. Several students really understand. After class they also ask me where they can do better. I know whether the student understands the course after just looking at his work, even if it is only a short time which lasts one or two hours.

媒介文化
Media Culture

Q：您课程的主要内容是？

A：主要是讲媒介文化作为一个概念的形成，就是它的来历。它是在——特别是电子文化产生以后，20世纪90年代以后，所有网络和电子技术的兴起所产生一种新的社会文化现象。总的来说课程包括三个内容：第一，微观媒介文化的基本理论；第二，关于文化时评和媒介批评的写作方法；第三，完成媒介批评论文。

Q: What is the main content of your course?

A: It mainly talks about the formation of media culture as a concept, which is its origin. It is a new social and cultural phenomenon arising from the emergence of all networks and electronic technologies, especially after the emergence of electronic culture in the 1990s. Generally speaking, the course includes three contents. The first is the basic theory of micro-media culture. The second is the writing methods of both cultural review and media criticism. And the third is the completion of papers about media criticism.

Q：您觉得这门课程的开设对于学生有什么意义？

A：我觉得同学们应该更加了解我们的现在，也就是我们现在所处的文化环境，知道应该如何看待正在我们周围发生的文化现象。它同古典文化不一样，古典文化基本上存在于纸面上，存在于我们的课本里面，但是媒介文化是在我们的生活中间，在我们的电脑上。

Q: What do you think is the significance of this course for students?

A: I think students should have a better understanding of our present, that is, the cultural environment we are in now, and know how to look upon the cultural phenomena that are taking place around us. It is different from classical culture. Classical culture basically exists on paper and in our textbooks. But media culture is in our lives and in our computer.

领略神奇的 AR 技术

Getting to Know AR

Q：您为什么会选择 AR 作为主要教学内容？

A：我想我们实验室一贯以来的特点，就是把一些比较前沿的技术与艺术创作的过程结合起来，把这些大家平时可能很少有机会动手去做的东西变得比较简单，两天里面可以完成，然后让所有专业的同学都可以体验。所以我们这次开设了这门课程，选择了增强现实的手段作为课程的主题。

Q: Why do you choose AR as the main teaching content?

A: I think our laboratory has always been characterized by the combination of some relatively cutting-edge technologies with the process of artistic creation. I make it easy to do things that students may seldom have the chance to do by themselves. And it can be done in two days. I let the students of all majors experience. So I offer this course, and choose augmented reality as the theme of the course.

Q：您觉得这门课程对于学生来说有什么意义？

A：我觉得，让学生对我们现在整个数字媒体艺术领域的科技创造形式的前沿有一些了解，一直以来就是我们做这一系列工作坊的一个目的，就是说让大家有机会接触到一些不同的东西，开阔一下视野，这是第一个。第二个很重要的意义在于，让学生对这些东西，不再排斥、不再畏惧，甚至产生一些兴趣。因为学生都是来自不同专业，不一定都是动画专业的，有些同学可能会觉得这些东西跟他无关，或者觉得很可怕，好像只能别人做我自己做不了。那么通过两天的时间，虽然不可能从头到尾完整地讲解完一个软件的操作，或者说学习一个完整的课程，但是我们能够把相关内容浓缩到两天里面来，让学生可以自己动手做一遍，相信有了这次的成果以后，下次再接触类似的项目就不会害怕了。下次要做某一个项目，比如说广告专业的学生要策划一次商业活动，或者传播学专业的学生希望去尝试一种新的传播手段，或者就可以考虑用 AR 技术来做。这可能是除了让大家开阔眼界以外，第二个很重要的目标。

Q: What do you think is the significance of this course for students?

A: In my opinion, it has always been one of the purposes of this series of workshops to give students some insight into the frontiers of technological creation in the whole field of digital media art. That is to say, our purpose is to offer everyone access to something different and broaden their horizons. This is the first significance. The second one is to stop students rejecting and fearing these things, and even take interest in them. Because students are from different majors, namely, some of them do not major in animation. Some students may feel that these things have nothing to do with them. Or they feel terrible, and they think that only others can do but they cannot do it themselves. So in two days, although it is impossible to fully explain the operation of a software from beginning to end, or to learn a complete course, we can condense the relevant content into two days so that students can do it by themselves. I believe that with this result, next time when students come into contact with similar projects, they will not be afraid. Next time when they want to do a project, for example, if students majoring in advertising want to plan a business activity, or students majoring in communication want to try a new means of communication, maybe they can consider using AR technology to do it. This may be the second important goal besides broadening their horizons.

工作坊日志一页 17 级动画 张锦雯

The page of workshop log Zhang Jinwen, a student majoring in animation of Grade 2017

集萃 Treasury

树脂立体画

3D Resin Painting

学生感言："莎莎老师很温柔，会耐心地指导我们，帮我们灌胶，甚至在我不小心弄倒胶时，也没有责怪我。在制作过程中，老师还会拿出蓝牙音响，让我们听音乐，整个教室的氛围也因此特别融洽，把一项任务、作业，真正变成了一种享受。"

A student said: "The teacher by the name of Liao Shasha is very gentle. She patiently guided us, and helped us pour glue. She didn't blame me even when I accidentally knocked down the glue. In the production process, the teacher took out the Bluetooth stereo to play music for us. The atmosphere of the whole classroom is particularly harmonious. It really turns a task and assignment into a kind of enjoyment."

学生感言："真的很喜欢莎莎老师，即使我们的想法十分天马行空，有时对待器具还有点粗心大意，她都一直耐心亲切，也可爱地和我们开玩笑。大家是在一种轻松、愉悦的环境下进行自己的创作，即使回去的时候已经是深夜了，我们依然甘之如饴。"

A student said: "I really like the teacher by the name of Liao Shasha. Even though our ideas were very unrestrained and sometimes we were a little careless about the appliances, she was always patient and kind, and made jokes with us lovingly. We worked in a relaxed and pleasant environment. Even though it was late at night when we returned, we were still happy."

"课程一共是两天的时间。在这两天里，同学们需要完成一共四层的树脂绘画。课程分为四部分，分别在每天的早上和晚上授课，一堂课完成一层的绘画。每次都是先画一层，调好树脂胶，把它灌上去，晾干。晾干之后，下堂课又再画一层，采用相同的工序。在炎炎夏日中，同学们耐下性子、安静地坐在实验室里仔细打磨自己的工艺品。我想通过这门课程，引导同学对待创作更加耐心，戒骄戒躁，同时修身养性。"——授课教师点评

17 级广播电视编导 宁静

Ning Jing, a student majoring in Radio and Television Editor of Grade 2017

"The course lasts two days. In these two days, students need to complete a total four layers of resin painting. The course is divided into four parts, which are taught in the morning and evening respectively. Students need to complete one layer of painting in one class. Every time students draw a layer first, adjust the resin glue, pour it on and dry it. After drying, draw another layer in the next class, and use the same process. In hot summer, students sit in the laboratory quietly and patiently, carefully polishing their own crafts. Through this course, I want to guide students to be more patient with creation, guard against arrogance and rashness, and cultivate their self-cultivation at the same time."

——Comments of the teacher

17 级广告 孙世鹏

Sun Shipeng, a student majoring in Advertising of Grade 2017

学生感言："左边是一只海獭，我是分成四层去做的。第一层只是打底，是黑色的；之后是第二层加毛、加腿、放眼，之后确定一个眼睛的位置；第三层就是细致的填充；第四层最后把鼻子画上。右边是一只小猫咪，跟画海獭的步骤差不多，因为有点空，我加了一个毛绒绒的线球。"

A student said: "It's a sea otter on the left. I made it in four layers. The first layer is just the bottoming, and it's black. For the second layer, hair, legs and eyes are added, and the position of eyes is determined. The third layer is meticulous filling. The fourth layer is to draw the nose finally. On the right it's a kitten. The steps of drawing the kitten is similar to that of drawing the sea otter."

木版水印

Chinese Traditional Watercolor Woodblock Printing

学生感言："回顾一天的学习，实实在在感受到了木版艺术的魅力，也由衷地敬佩工艺制作者。一块精美的水印需要制作者严密的逻辑思维去设计、极高的审美能力去填充，着实凝聚了制作者的一番苦心。在自己不断尝试之后，看到'月夜'的雏形逐渐完善，即使最终的作品不尽如人意，但还是非常有成就感。"

A student said: "Looking back on one day's study, I really feel the charm of woodblock art. I also sincerely admire the craftsmen. An exquisite watermark needs the producer's strict logical thinking to design and high aesthetic ability to fill, which really condenses the producer's pains. After continuing to try, I saw the prototype of 'Moon Night' gradually improved. Even though the final work is not satisfactory, I still feel very accomplished."

学生感言："第一次接触木版水印。一开始老师问有没有绘画基础，我以为跟绘画有很大的关系，自己真正上手之后，才发现更多的是需要耐心与专心。只有褪去毛躁，将内心沉稳下来，才能刻好自己的画。内心真正平和，就不会觉得很难了，反而会收获非常多的乐趣。"

A student said: "It' my first exposure to watercolor woodblock printing. At the beginning the teacher asked if we had some painting background, I thought that it had a lot to do with painting. After I really started, I found that it needed patience and concentration more. Only when we get rid of our impatience and calm down can we carve our own pictures well. When I feel peaceful in mind, I will not find it difficult, but have a lot of fun instead."

17 级广播电视编导 宁静

Ning Jing, a student majoring in Radio and Television Editor of Grade 2017

学生感言："通过两天的学习，我对事情的专注度以及耐心有着显著的提高。因为一不小心就会被刻刀划破伤口，而丧失耐心的时候，作品也会变得毛毛躁躁。就像一幅好的木版水印需要经过一次次耐心地打磨一样，任何事情少了专注度与耐心都无法很好地完成。感谢费老师，通过两天的课程让我明白了任何事情都不是随随便便就能成功的，背后一定要付出百分百，甚至更多的努力。"

A student said: "Through two days of study, my focus and patience on things have improved significantly. Because if I am not careful, I will be cut by a carving knife. And when I lose patience, my works will become impatient. Just as a good watercolor woodblock printing needs to be patiently polished over and over again, nothing can be done well without concentration and patience. Thank you, Mr. FEI. Through the two-day course, I learned that nothing can be achieved casually, that there must be 100% or even more effort behind it."

"做木版水印最难的就是控制水分。制作过程中纸和木板都是湿的，水分一旦没控制好，印的时候就会损坏，失败率其实还是挺高的。但同学们不断从中汲取教训，最终交上来的作品还是很出效果的。"

——授课教师点评

"The most difficult part of doing watercolor woodblock printing is to control water content. Paper and boards are wet in the production process. Once the moisture is not controlled well, the printing will be damaged. In fact, the failure rate is quite high. But students continue to draw lessons from it, and the final works handed in are quite effective."

——Comments of the teacher

中国书法

Chinese Calligraphy

学生感言：“中国书法是中华文明的结晶，尽管我们生活在一个高科技的时代，快节奏的生活会让我们抛弃、丢失很多东西，但不应该将中华文化的精华遗忘在历史的角落里。在学习生活中，可以时常练练字，传承这门艺术文化。”

A student said: “Chinese calligraphy is the crystallization of Chinese civilization. Although we live in a hi-tech era, fast-paced life will let us discard and lose a lot of things, but we should not leave the essence of Chinese culture in the corner of history. During our college days, we can often practice Chinese calligraphy, and inherit this art and culture.”

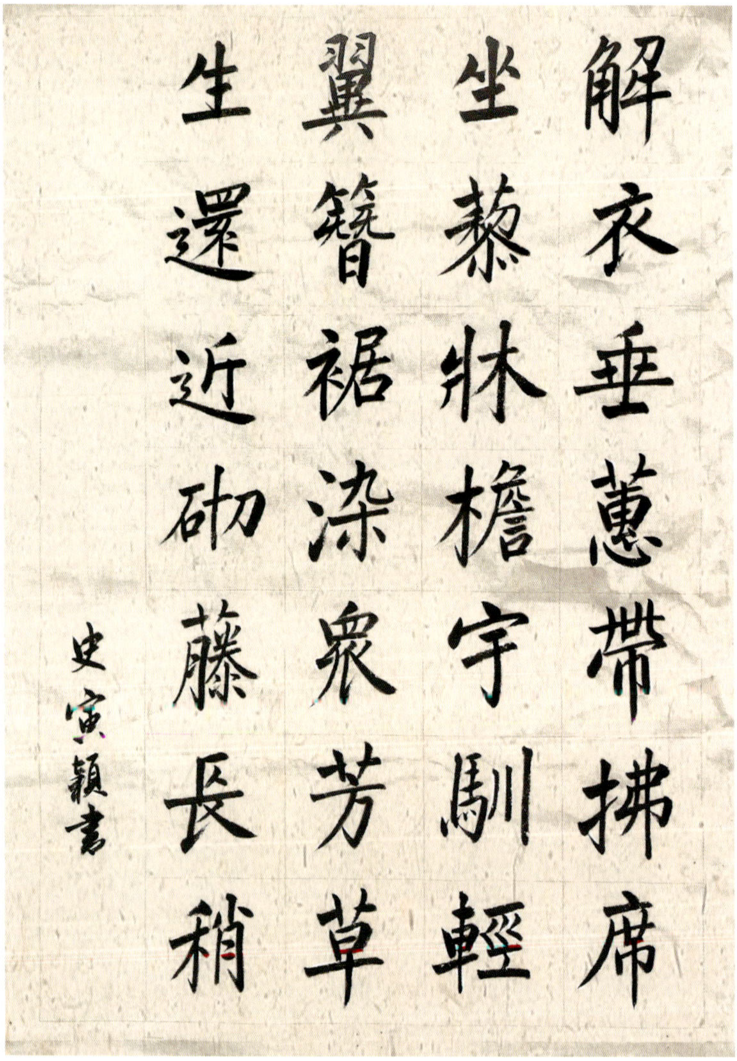

17级广播电视学 史寅颖

Shi Yinying, a student majoring in Radio and Television Science of Grade 2017

学生感言：“在两天的时间中，我们学习了篆、隶、楷等书体，临摹了颜真卿、王羲之等名家的字帖，体会了不同的书写风格，如隶书的规整、行楷的流畅等，还临摹了一些知名学府的校名。在这个手机不可或缺的时代，书法帮助我们摆脱了手机的束缚，获得了心灵的宁静，好不惬意！”

A student said: “During the two days, we learned seal scripts, official scripts and regular scripts. We copied the posts of famous writers such as Yan Zhenqing and Wang Xizhi. We have personally learned different writing styles, such as the neatness of official scripts, the fluency of regular scripts, and so on. We also copied the names of some famous universities. In this era when mobile phones are indispensable, calligraphy helps us get rid of the shackles of mobile phones, and find the peace of mind. It's very pleasant!”

“书法可以说是我们国粹中的国粹。书法应该在所有的文化、所有的语言、所有的书写中都存在，但唯独中国书法独具魅力。我之前在其他的985大学乃至美术院校上课，都是至少半年、一年、两年时间讲理论，讲书法美学，讲书法史，还讲书法技巧，现在浓缩到两天时间，初时感到很惶然，却有意想不到的收获。同学们很多是零起点，书法写作却有飞速的提升。”

——授课教师点评

“Calligraphy can be said to be the quintessence of our country. Calligraphy is supposed to exist in all cultures, languages and writings. But only Chinese calligraphy has its unique charm. I have taught in other “985” universities and even art colleges for at least half a year, one year or two years on theory, aesthetics of calligraphy, history of calligraphy, and skills of calligraphy. Now it's condensed to two days. At first I felt very nervous, but I got unexpected harvest. The starting point of many students is zero, but their writing of calligraphy has been improved by leaps and bounds.”

——Comments of the teacher

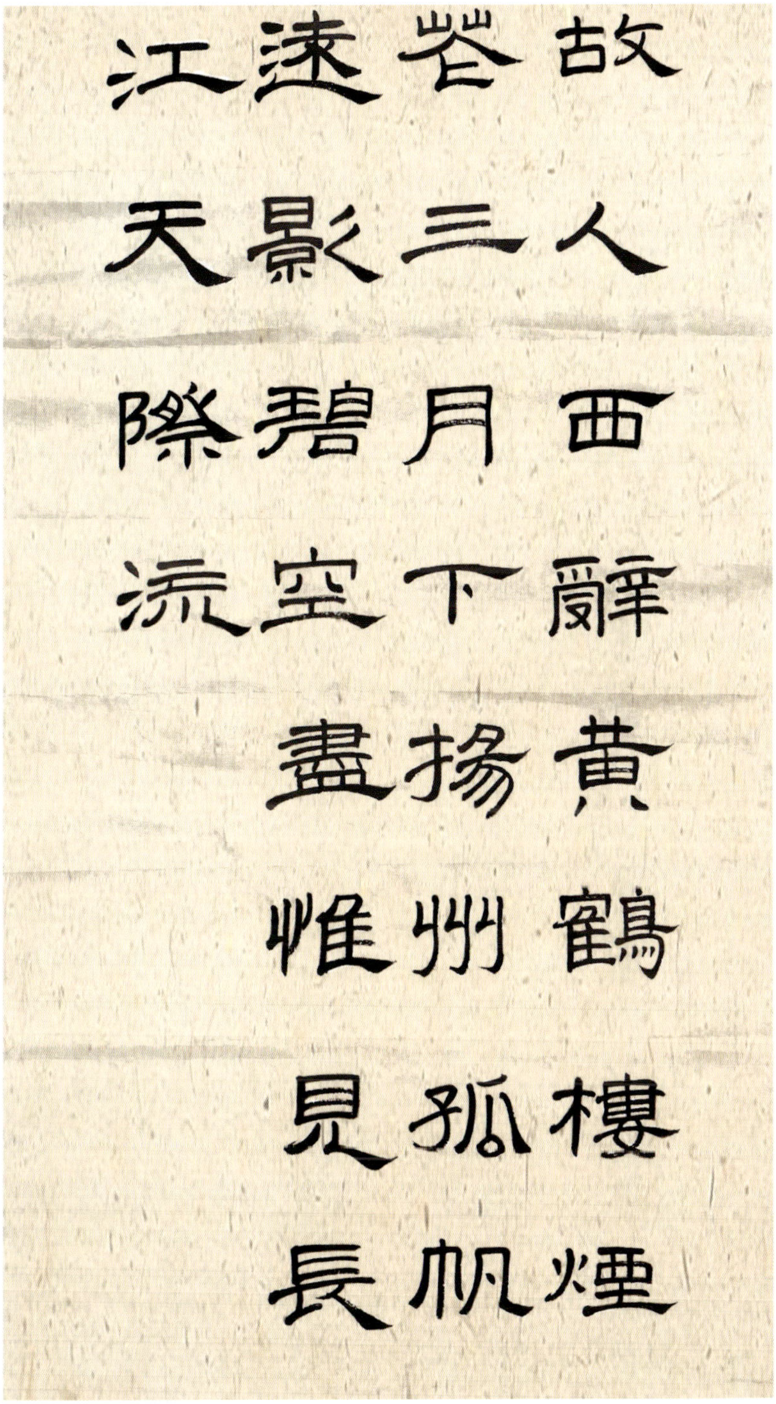

17级广播电视编导 范斯晶

Fan Sijing, a student majoring in Radio and Television Editor of Grade 2017

版式与色彩设计

Format and Color Design

学生感言："在小组的成品展示上，同学们都表现了自己的创意。新闻专业的同学以其独特的空间感，将同一颜色通过不同的排版，形成具有美感的韵律。动画专业的同学熟练地运用自己所掌握的知识，坚持自己的创作目的，虽然每一个人都被颜色的搭配折磨不已，但最终都出色地完成了自己的作品。"

A student said: "In the display of group's finished products, the students showed their creativity. Students majoring in journalism, with their unique sense of space, use the same color through different typesetting to form a rhythm with aesthetic feeling. Students majoring in animation use their knowledge skillfully and stick to their creative purposes. Although everyone was tormented by the matching of colors, they finished their works well in the end."

17 级广播电视编导 张越淇

Zhang Yueqi, a student majoring in Radio and Television Editor of Grade 2017

"在我看来，设计是面向市场的美术工程。好的设计作品不是孤芳自赏就够了。向由老师感慨的那样，'设计，离不开艺术，离不开技术，离不开营销'。以人为本是永恒不变的设计理念，受众是设计着眼的核心。通俗地说，作品得卖得出去。但这也不意味着设计作品就要去讨好受众。作品需要有烟火气，但绝不能媚俗化。"

A student said: "In my opinion, design is a market-oriented art project. A good design is not enough for self-admiration. As Teacher YOU said with emotion: 'Design cannot be separated from art, technology and marketing'. People-oriented is the eternal design concept, and audience is the core of the design. Generally speaking, the works have to be sold. But it doesn't mean that design works have to please the audience. Works need to be worldly, but they must not be vulgarized."

17 级动画 章轶文

Zhang Yiwen, a student majoring in Animation of Grade 2017

17 级动画 林芷萱

Lin Zhixuan, a student majoring in Animation of Grade 2017

“本次课程是进行界面设计中的版式布局和色彩设计的实践演练，通过自己研发的色彩和版式设计实践工具，同学进行了大量的创作尝试，在最终作品中展示了独特的风格和不同维度空间的感知探索。同学投入了很大热情，体现出不同的创作视角，最终作品出乎我的预计，也出乎很多同学自身的意料之外，发现不同的自己。”

——授课教师点评

“This course is the layout of interface design, and the practice of color design. Through the color they research and develop themselves, and practical tools for format design, students have made a lot of creative attempts. In the final work they show a unique style and perception exploration of space of different dimensions.”

——Comments of the teacher

品牌策划与活动设计
Brand Scheme and Activity Design

学生感言："在这门课中，王建民老师给予了我们很大的帮助。他是一位对于智能汽车以及新媒体了解很深的老师，在我们没有主见时，他会帮助我们打开思路，并指导我们选择快捷的、正确的方向。在过程中我十分享受小组合作的过程，尽管有争论与摩擦，但这种形式可以提高工作的效率。我在之后的课程中也会吸收相关的经验，争取继续提高自己的专业知识水平。"

A student said: "In this course, Professor Wang Jianmin has given us great help. He knows a lot about smart cars and new media. When we have no opinions, he helps us open our minds and guides us to choose the right direction quickly. I enjoy the process of group cooperation very much. Despite controversies and frictions, this form of work can improve efficiency. I will also absorb relevant experience in the following courses, and strive to continue to improve my professional knowledge level."

学生感言："王建民老师丰富的关于智能汽车及其竞赛活动的知识讲解和他充分准备的资料，给我打开了一个新的从未了解的领域。这种知识的新鲜感深深地吸引着我。智能汽车本身应用了很多前沿的高新技术，综合了许多知识。"

A student said: "The knowledge explanation from Professor Wang Jianmin, which is about smart cars and related competition activities, and his well-prepared information opened up a new field for me that I never knew before. The novelty of this knowledge attracts me deeply. Smart cars have applied many advanced high and new technologies, and synthesized a lot of knowledge."

LOGO 理念：我们创作设计的音乐 LOGO 是降 D 大调。在音乐的调式中，大调具有明亮的色彩，与赛车驾驶者热情向上的精神密切相关。在大小调体系中，Ⅰ、Ⅲ、Ⅴ级都是稳定音级。我们采用的调式，奠定了一个稳定、平衡、发展的作曲风格。在配器上，我们采用了金属鼓并加以电子音乐的元素，强有力，具有节奏感、现代感。

主题曲理念：电子音乐作为音乐艺术与科学技术的跨界产物，在人类艺术史的发展进程中占据重要位置，而智能汽车也是科学技术的体现，因此我们用电子音乐与汽车融合，一刚一柔，以表现出赛车的磅礴气势，贴近本次活动表达的精神。

LOGO concept: Our music LOGO is in D flat major. In the mode of music, major has bright color, which is closely related to the enthusiasm and upward spirit of racing drivers. In major and minor system, I, III and V are stable. The mode we adopted established a stable, balanced and developing composing style. In the orchestration, we use metal drums and electronic music elements, which are powerful and carries a sense of rhythm and modernity.

Theme song concept: As a cross-border product of music art and science and technology, electronic music plays an important role in the development of human art history. Smart cars are also the embodiment of science and technology. Therefore, we integratively use electronic music and cars, one rigid and one soft, to show the grand momentum of racing cars, which is close to the spirit expressed in this event.

学生感言：“通过这门课，我学习到很多与本专业相关的知识，例如一个活动的准备需要从策划开始，一步一步到最终完成，其实在背后付出的人很多。在生活中我们是表演者，总觉得自己已经很辛苦，现在才知道，每一个策划都是通过一个又一个的通宵实现的，每一个环节的负责人更是为了寻找素材面临一次又一次的失败，最终才能有一个完美的舞台呈现。虽然只有两天的课程，但是意义很深刻。”

A student said: “Through this course, I learned a lot of knowledge related to my major. For example, the preparation of an activity needs to start from planning to the final completion step by step. In fact, there are many people behind it. In our daily life we are performers, and we always feel life isn't easy for us. Now I know that every plan is done through all-night work one by one. In order to find the material, the leaders of each link experienced repeated failures. Only in the end can they have a perfect stage presentation. Although it’s only two-day course, it’s of profound significance.”

“两天的课程围绕当下智能汽车的学生竞赛活动的策划展开。学生分为 4 个小组，从活动策划、媒体策划、展演活动、音乐创作进行分组和集体讨论，分工协作。4 个团队的同学分别来自音乐、表演、广告、新闻专业，他们都带有本身的专业背景知识，相对独立地完成策划案的一部分。团队之间还需要相互协作，完成嘉年华策划活动方案的完整报告。课程成果包含：‘高校智能卡丁车大赛——汽车嘉年华活动’策划案、运营方案，以及相关的新媒体创作，包含主题声音设计、主题海报设计、主题品牌活动 LOGO 设计等内容。”

——授课教师点评

“The two-day course revolves around the planning of the current student competition for smart cars. Students are divided into the following four groups: planning of activities, media planning, exhibition activities, and music creation. Students discuss together, divide their work and cooperate. The students of the four teams major in music, performance, advertising and journalism. They all have their own knowledge of professional background, and they relatively independently complete part of the plan. Teams also need to work together to complete a whole report on the carnival planning activities. The results of the course include: the scheme and operational plan of 'Smart Carding Competition in Colleges and Universities–Carnival of Automobiles' and related new media creation, including theme voice design, theme poster design, theme brand activity LOGO design and so on.”

——Comments of the teacher

展览设计快速入门到实践

Exhibition Design from Quick Start to Practice

学生感言："汪家羽老师作为笔克公司的创意总监，讲的东西很专业很精彩，很快就让我们投入这门课程中。这门课对我而言要点在创意，而创意是我们这个年龄最应该思考的东西，不得不说创意对我来说是一个不小的挑战。"

A student said: "As the creative director of Bike Company, Mr. Wang Jiayu gave us very professional and wonderful lectures, which let us devote ourselves to this course very soon. The main point of this course for me is creativity, which is the most important thing to think about in our age. I have to say that creativity is a big challenge for me."

学生感言："好的展台设计应当抓住受众心理，最重要的是设计一个符合自己想要抓住的群体心理的主题，并将其运用到极致。在整个创意构思的过程中，我们对于主题的确立并不是非常清晰，导致在后续执行的过程中，逐渐偏离了原来的构想，甚至几乎全部推倒重来。这也是我在之后的工作和学习中应当注意的地方。最好在创意构思阶段就将所有的问题都考虑好，而不是在执行过程中再发现和修改。"

A student said: "Good exhibition booth design should affract the audience. The most important thing is to design a theme that meets the group's psychology that you want to grasp, and apply it to the extreme. In the whole creative process, we were not very clear about the establishment of the theme, resulting in the follow-up implementation process, gradually deviating from the original idea. We almost had to push over to do it again. This is what I should pay attention to in my future work and study. It's better to take all the issues into consideration at the creative stage than to rediscover and modify them in the process of implementation."

1. "潮路"通道示例

2. "变装"通道

学生作品 张信真、丁熙桐、佟心、徐舟爽、张兴泰

Students' works Zhang Xizhen, Ding Xitong, Tong Xin, Xu Zhoushuang, Zhang Xingtai

大会形象装置/主舞台区

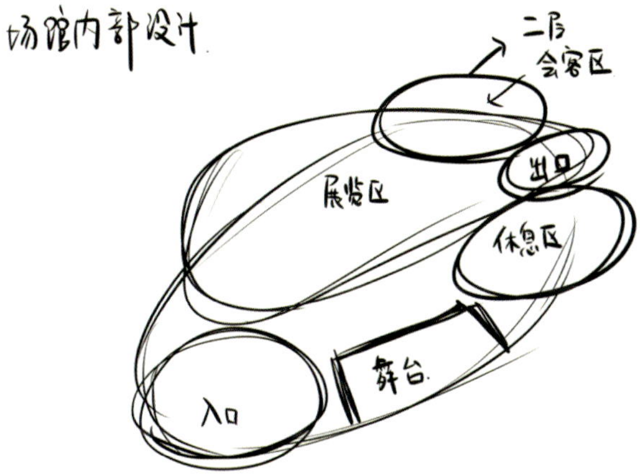

学生作品 张僖真、丁熙桐、佟心、徐舟爽、张兴泰

Students' works Zhang Xizhen, Ding Xitong, Tongxin, Xu Zhoushuang, Zhang Xingtai

“我们学生的专业跨度真的很大，从动画、广编、广告学到音乐还有表演，每一个同学都做一个作品出来是不现实的，每个人选的东西也不一样。所以我想发挥他们各自的特长，四个人一个小组，每个小组里面会有不同专业学生，大家共同完成课题。课程需要广编关于新闻策划方面的内容，需要广告学对于一些主视觉元素的把握，需要动画专业的人把它建成一个真正的三维造型，也需要音乐和表演系来提供一些表演方面的建议，很多展览展示活动都有现场的表演。我很希望借此普及展览展示的知识。展览展示是一个一比九的经济，具有很强的经济价值和社会责任价值，国家也大力在扶持推广，会是一个很有前景的行业。”

——授课教师点评

“Our students' majors span a lot, including animation, radio and television editor, advertising, music and performance. It is unrealistic for every student to make a work. Everyone chooses different things. So I want to give full play to their respective strengths. There are four people in every group. In every group students are from different majors. They work together to complete the project. In the course, students from radio and television editor plan the contents of news, students from advertising grasp some of the main visual elements, students from animation build a real three-dimensional model, and students from music and performance provide some suggestions on performance. There is live performance in many exhibitions. I would like to take this opportunity to popularize the knowledge of displaying in the exhibition. Exhibition is a one-to-nine economy with strong economic value and social responsibility value. The country is also vigorously supporting the promotion of it, and it will be a promising industry.”

——Comments of the teacher

延时摄影

Time-Lapse Photography

学生感言："在努力了解 LR 和 LRT 软件后，把将近 40G 的素材导成视频格式，看到汗流浃背拍过来的延时镜头浓缩成三十几秒的视频，我们着实为其震撼。拍摄过程本身就是一种享受。坐在图书馆 10 楼的窗前，凉风徐徐拂面，夕阳透过三脚架进入我们的视线，在快节奏的生活中难得的慢了下来，也许这就是延时摄影的魅力。"

A student said: "After trying to understand LR and LRT software. We transformed nearly 40G of material into video format. We were really shocked to see delay lens shot in sweat back condensed into the video of more than 30 seconds. The process of shooting itself is a kind of enjoyment. Sitting in front of the window on the 10th floor of the library, the cool wind slowly brushes our faces and the sunset enters our sight through the tripod. It's rare to slow down in a fast-paced life. Maybe that's the charm of time-lapse photography."

学生感言："大家一起从下午拍到晚上月亮挂上月梢，我们撑着伞坐在行李上还得保持不动，路人诧异的眼神也让我觉得非常不自在。但是当成果出来，感觉一切都值了。"

A student said: "We work from afternoon to evening when the moon hangs on the treetops. We sat on our luggage with an umbrella and had to stay still. The surprised eyes of passers-by also made me feel very uncomfortable. But when the rusult comes out, it feels like everything's worth it."

夏仕欣、王翊萌

Xia Shixin, Wang Yimeng

"这门课和其他课程最主要的不同就是需要晚上操作。因为这是一个时间积累的过程：拍一组镜头至少需要两小时，那么三组镜头至少要花六小时去拍，还有很多限制，比如拍日落必须在日落时分，拍日出必须在凌晨，拍星星必须在晚上，拍灯光也要在晚上……我相信当同学们进入创作阶段的时候，他们就开始真正走上专业人士所走的道路了。"

——授课教师点评

"The main difference between this course and other courses is that it needs to be operated at night. Because it's a process of time accumulation. It takes at least two hours to shoot one set of shots, and at least six hours to shoot three sets of shots. There are many limitations. For example, sunset must be taken at sunset, sunrise must be taken at dawn, stars and lights must be taken at night. I believe that when students enter the creative stage, they begin to really embark on the path of professionals."

——Comments of the teacher

李欣然、张越淇

Li Xinran, Zhang Yueqi

薛亮、章傲涵、陶以诺、刘杨、徐英男

Xue Liang, Zhang Aohan, Tao Yinuo, Liu Yang, Xu Yingnan

“同学们的作品看起来时长很短，实际上在拍摄时至少需要固定在一个景点两小时，更不用说还有后期的剪辑——不仅只是镜头的拼接，转场、音乐的搭配都十分重要。这门课程对我们来说是一种积累，虽然熬夜过后很疲惫，但作品是用心做出来的，成就感很高。”

——授课教师点评

“The students' works seem to be very short. In fact, they need to be fixed in a scenic spot for at least two hours when shooting, let alone the later editing. Not only the splicing of shots, but also the transition and the music matching are very important. This course is accumulation for us. Although tired after staying up late, We put our heart into the work and had a great sense of achievement.”

——Comments of the teacher

特效摄影与高速摄影

Special Effects & High-speed Photography

学生感言：“薛航老师是位非常帅气的人，无论是说话还是做事都果断高效，谈吐间充满了个人魅力，对我们的行为不时来点吐槽，让大家都开心地笑了起来。我个人非常喜欢这种课堂氛围，让人愿意积极投入其中。”

A student said: “Mr. XUE Hang is very handsome. He is decisive and efficient in both speaking and doing things. His speech and manner are full of personal charm. Sometime he joked about our behavior, and made everybody laugh happily. Personally I like this kind of classroom atmosphere very much, because are willing to actively participate in it.”

学生感言：“有魅力的事物往往只存在那么一瞬间，用心去关注，抓住最好的刹那。这个过程需要些许运气，但更多的是保证自己的专注度和耐心。经历过一次又一次失败后，终能获得一张精彩的瞬间。”

A student said: “Charming things often exist only for a moment. Attend with heart, seize the best moment. This process requires a little luck, but our concentration and patience is more required. After numerous failures, we can finally get a wonderful moment.”

陈佳音

Chen Jiayin

司舒舒

Si Shushu

庞猗箐

Pang Yijing

许芯蕾

Xu Xinlei

“金鱼是很难抓拍的，我们经常拍到的是它们在半空中或者触底，这都是很实际的问题。而我们需要去锻炼抓时机的方法。如庞猗箐同学的这幅照片，金鱼在水里面展开了姿态，同时水花也溅起。”

——授课教师点评

“Goldfish is hard to capture on the camera. We often photograph them in mid-air or touching the bottom. These are all practical problems. And we need to practice ways to seize the moment. In this photo by Pang Yiqing, the goldfish gestures in the water and the water splashes at the same time.”

——Comments of the teacher

17 级广播电视学 张宇昭

Zhang Yuzhao, a student majoring in Radio and Television Science of Grade 2017

“大家平时应该没有仔细观察过火的形态，而这张照片其实是给我们提供了一个全新的视角——这是一个非常饱满的火焰形态。”

——授课教师点评

“You may not have carefully observed the shape of the fire, but this photo actually provides us with a new perspective. This is a very full flame form.”

——Comments of the teacher

17 级广播电视学 许芯蕾

Xu Xinlei, a student majoring in Radio and Television Science of Grade 2017

17 级广播电视学 王晴

Wang Qing, a student majoring in Radio and Television Science of Grade 2017

“在一些不经意的瞬间，火会呈现出让人充满想象的画面。这幅照片就是展示这样一个瞬间，仿佛凤凰展翅。”

——授课教师点评

“In some inadvertent moments, fire will present a picture full of imagination. This picture shows such a moment, like a phoenix spreading its wings.”

——Comments of the teacher

网络短视频制作
The Production of Internet Videos

学生感言：“近两年短视频迅速发展，成为人们众多娱乐生活方式中的一种。短视频最大的特点就是有趣与有用，它表意直接，构图简洁，以语言、字幕为主，音乐与音效为辅。课上我们不仅学会了一款新的视频处理软件的使用，结束时还创作出了自己的短视频，收获满满。”

A student said: “Short videos have developed rapidly in recent two years and become one of the entertainment lifestyles of people. The most striking feature of short videos is that they are interesting and useful. It is direct in meaning and concise in composition. It is based on language and subtitles, supplemented by music and sound effects. In class, we not only learned how to use a new video processing software, but also created our own short videos at the end of the lesson. We have a lot of harvest.”

学生作品 Shanghai View 王宇

Students' work *Shanghai View* Wang Yu

“课程要求学生在规定时间（10 小时）内最大程度地实现创意，制作有意思的网络短视频，鼓励跨专业合作。最终作业类型丰富，有致敬网红短视频的《割盲肠》《杠精教学》等；尝试镜头组接技巧的《嘉定一日游》“Shanghai view”；探索声画的“Live it up”；致力原创的《好妹妹说电影》《优雅插花》《母女日常》等；利用网络素材加工的恶搞类型《中国队勇夺世界杯》等。大家都很踊跃，也都很有兴趣。我第一轮作业给他们提了三种可参考的类型，在制作过程当中，有同学发展出了第四种类型，但未能实现，第二轮作业时我有意识地提醒了他们，最终有同学做出了第四种，这种螺旋式进步的态势就很好。音乐和表演专业的同学虽然没有学过视频制作，但在创意方面毫不逊色，有自己的专业优势和特色。说实话同学们的创意更有活力，或者说更有趣味性，有些作业我觉得都具有成为网红的潜力。我自己还是第一次开设这门课程，我觉得很有意义，以后可能还会继续。”

——授课教师点评

“The course requires students to maximize their creativity within the prescribed time (10 hours), make interesting short online videos, and encourage cross-professional cooperation. There are many types of final assignments, including those saluting short video of internet celebrity such as *Cecumectomy* and *Contrarian Teaching*, those trying lens assembly techniques such as *Shanghai View*, those exploring sound and picture such as *Live it up*, those dedicated to originality such as *Good Sister Talks about Movies*, *Elegant Flower Arrangement* and *Daily life of Mother and Daughter*, those kind of spoof processing with network materials such as *Chinese Win the World Cup*, etc. Everyone is enthusiastic and interested. I gave them three types of reference in my first round of homework. In the process of production, some students developed the fourth type, but failed to achieve it. In the second round of homework, I consciously reminded them, and eventually some students made the fourth one. This trend of spiral progress is very good. Although students majoring in music and performance had not studied video production, they are not inferior in creativity and they have their own professional advantages and characteristics. To be honest, students' creativity is more dynamic, or more interesting. I think that some work has the potential to become internet celebrity. It's my first time to offer this course. I think it's very meaningful and I may continue to do it in the future.”

——Comments of the teacher

影视作品的声音设计
Sound Design for Film and Video

学生感言："这门课更多地带给我一种对于影视作品剪辑制作、传达创作者意图的新思路。在技术实现方面，老师引入专门的声音编辑软件，但最终声画合成工作依赖工作者平时的掌握。不同的是，新思维与老方法的结合带来了令人惊喜的变化。以往在 pr 中剪片子，更注重画面，常出现视轨七八个、音轨一两个的情况。在这次学习中，音轨数量多起来，也是影片在这一方面更有层次的最直观体现。"

A student said: "This course gives me a new way to edit and produce film and television works and to convey the intention of the creator. In the aspect of technical realization, the teacher introduced a special voice editing software, but ultimately the work of sound and picture synthesis relies on the creator's knowledge. The difference is that the combination of new thinking and old methods has brought about surprising changes. In the past when we do film cutting in pr, we pay more attention to the screen. Often there are seven or eight visual tracks, and one or two audio tracks. In this course, the number of audio tracks has increased. It is also the most intuitive manifestation of hierarchy of the film in this aspect."

学生感言："对于一部作品而言，声音是必不可少的环节。我第一次接触到影视的后期声效，也第一次知道了原来大多数的声音是通过拟音来完成的，这让我感到十分不可思议，也对声音设计有了一个全新的认知。"

A student said: "For a work, sound is an indispensable aspect. It's the first time that I came into contact with the late sound effects of film and television. It's also the first time that I knew that most of the original sound was accomplished through onomatopoeia. It amazed me and gave me a new understanding of sound design."

17 级音乐表演 王艺颖

Wang Yiying, a student majoring in Music Performance of Grade 2017

17 级广播电视学 唐颖

Tang Ying, a student majoring in Radio and Television Science of Grade 2017

17 级广播电视编导 周丽

Zhou Li, a student majoring in Radio and Television Editor of Grade 2017

“课程开始跟同学们介绍了声音设计的概念和一些基本原理，通过经典的影片片段，让大家了解声音设计在这些片段里的作用。之后给他们挑了三段没有声音的影视片段，只提供声音的素材，让他们通过这些素材把声音加到影片里面去，最后出一个成品。成片制作完成会有演示环节，每个同学上台播放自己的作品，然后做一下点评。我希望他们通过实践对声音的后期制作有一个基本的理念并能运用到之后的个人作品中。”

——授课教师点评

“The course began by introducing the concepts and basic principles of sound design to the students. Through the classic film clips, I introduced the role of sound design in these clips to the students. After that, the students were given three silent video clips, which only provided sound material. The students were asked to add sound to the film through these materials, and finally produced a finished product. There was a demonstration when the production was completed. Each student came on stage to play his own work, and then made a comment. I hope they have a basic idea about the post-production of sound through practice, and they can apply it in their personal works in future.”

——Comments of the teacher

台词对白

Lines & Dialogues Lesson

学生感言："不同专业领域的结合让我们有了很多新鲜的感受。和我们一组的小姐姐有天生的镜头感，在表演时非常引人注目，她为了配合我们的视频拍摄展现了极高的专业能力，当然她也从中学到了一些拍摄剪辑以及修图的技巧。感谢这次工作坊让我的暑期小学期充满了乐趣。"

A student said: "The combination of different professional fields gives us a lot of fresh feelings. The innate sense of camera of the little sister in our group, is very eye-catching in the performance. She showed great professionalism in order to cooperate with our video shooting. Of course, she also learned some skills in shooting, editing and drawing revision. We'd like to thank the workshop for making my summer semester full of fun."

学生感言："以前对于'演技'这个概念的认识其实是很抽象的，而当我自己拿到台本，要去处理其中的情绪、表演技巧、动作调度的时候，才发现自己是多么的手足无措。这个时候再去看周、李二人对于角色的处理，真是会情不自禁地拍手叫绝！"

A student said: "Previously my understanding of the concept of 'acting' was very abstract. When I got the playscript with stage directions, I had to deal with the emotions, performance skills and movement scheduling, and I realized how bewildered I was. Then I see how Zhou and Li deal with their roles, I can't help clapping my hands and exclaiming!"

学生感言："饶老师先是仔细地向我们介绍了整篇故事的概况，再让我们自己体会人物的性格特点，找到人物的关键词去更好地诠释角色。经过两天的学习，我们真的得到了提升。台词的功底与表演一样重要，一个好的演员要经得起考验。整个班级的同学都被饶老师对于舞台的专注和认真所感染，非表演专业同学的演技也让我感到十分惊艳。"

A student said: "Ms Rao first introduced the whole story to us carefully, then let us understand the characteristics of the characters and find the key words of the characters to better interpret the roles. After two days study, we really got a promotion. The foundation of lines is as important as performance. A good actor must stand the test. Our whole class was infected by Ms Rao's dedication and seriousness to the stage. The acting skills of the students of non-performance major also amazed me."

“首先因为我们学院的女生特别多，男生比例是非常小的，所以挑选了《金枝欲孽》《雷雨》《风声》等经典剧目，设置了很多女性角色，可以满足学生的练习需求，另外，大家对这些剧目也比较熟悉。近年来清宫戏比较流行，很多同学都是从小看清宫戏长大的，所以他们入戏特别快，这就让他们能够很快建立起自信心。《金枝欲孽》是电视剧，《风声》是广有口碑的一个电影，同学们在对经典的演绎过程中很快会知道，其实经典是非常难的，它们的意义在哪里，以及就经典作品的训练目的和训练意义在哪里。”

——授课教师点评

“First of all, because there are a large number of female students in our college and a very small proportion of male students, I have selected some classic plays such as *Beauty at War*, *Thunderstorm*, *The Message* and so on. Many female roles are set up to meet the students' practice needs. In addition, we are familiar with these plays. In recent years, the drama about court life of the Qing Dynasty has become more popular. Many students grew up watching the drama from a young age, so they entered the drama very quickly, which enabled them to build up self-confidence quickly. *Beauty at War* is a TV play, and *The Message* is a movie with good reputation. Students will soon know the following in the process of deducing the classics: the classics are very difficult in fact, where their significance lies, as well as the training purpose and significance of the classics.”

——Comments of the teacher

影视特效化妆

Special Effects Make-up for Film and TV Works

学生感言："特效化妆是不会化妆的人了解化妆的一个很好的途径。老师会下来游走，指出我们的不足之处，手把手教我们化妆。在特效方面，我和老师进行了一次探讨，老师的一个观点令我印象深刻：在化妆时，哪怕只有一个镜头，妆容也要做到极致，绝不糊弄观众。我认为这种精益求精的态度是值得学习的。作为传媒专业学生，未来如果从事影视行业，自然每一个镜头、每一处细节都要做到最精致，要让自己的作品对得起观众。"

A student said: "Special effects make-up is a good way for people who can't make up to understand makeup. The teacher came down and walked around, pointed out our disadventages, and taught us how to make-up. In terms of special effects, I had a discussion with my teacher. I was impressed by the teacher's following point of view. In make-up, even if there is only one lens, make-up should be done to the utmost. Never fool the audience. I think this attitude of striving for excellence is worth learning. As a student majoring in media, if we want to be engaged in the film and television industry in the future, naturally every lens and every detail should be the most exquisite, so that our works can be worthy of the audience."

学生感言："两天的课程，让我这个化妆小白瞬间提升了很多。一开始说要互相化妆时，我生怕把搭档的脸画得不好。而我的搭档就不停地鼓励我，让我能大胆地在她的脸上进行创作。最后出来的成果让我们小小地惊艳了一把。"

A student said: "The two-day course, let me, a green hand of make-up, instantly improved a lot. At the beginning, when we were required to do each other's make-up, I was afraid that my partner's face would not be well made up. And my partner kept encouraging me to create on her face. The final result shocked us a little."

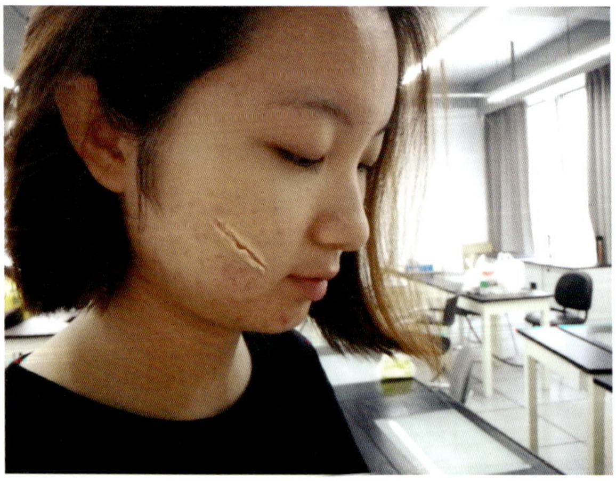

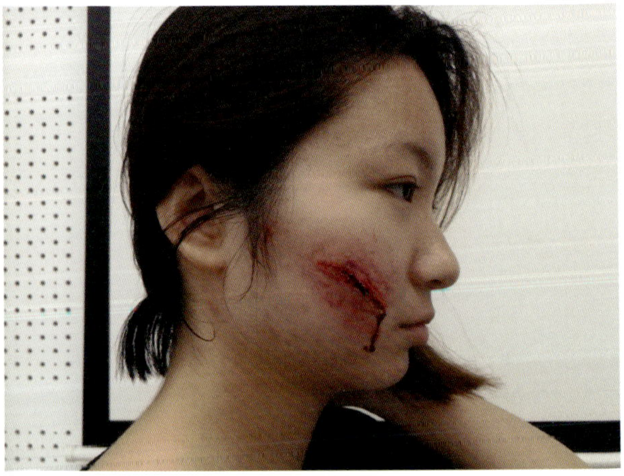

17级广播电视编导 卞丹亚

Bian Danya, a student majoring in Radio and Television Editor of Grade 2017

“特效化妆是一定要具备耐心的。我想鼓励学生不管做什么事情，千万不要中途放弃。你要去尝试，加上老师教给你的东西，再加上你的创意，就会呈现给大家不一样的东西，而这个东西是属于你自己的、别人带不走的。”

——授课教师点评

“Special effects make–up must be patient. I want to encourage students not to give up halfway no matter what they do. You need to try with what the teacher teaches you and your creativity. Something different will be shown finally. And this belongs to you and can't be taken away by others.”

——Comments of the teacher

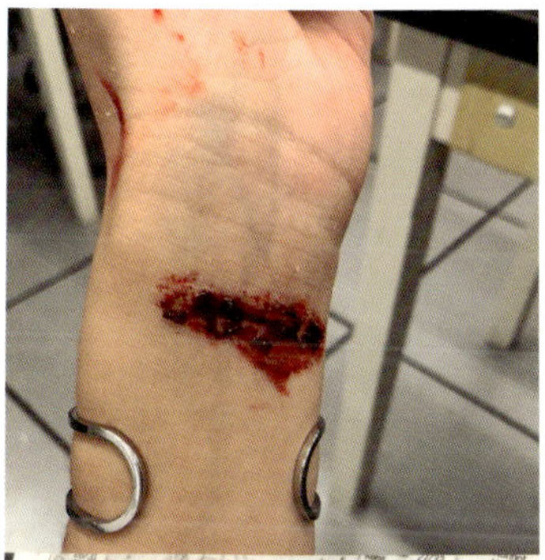

17 级广播电视学 江雪瑶

Jiang Xueyao, a student majoring in Radio and Television Science of Grade 2017

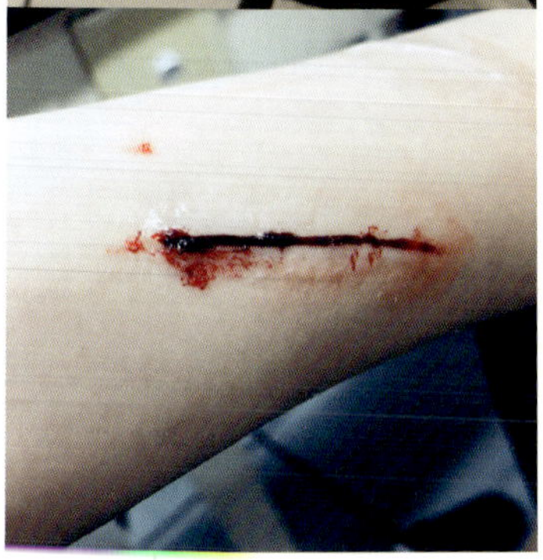

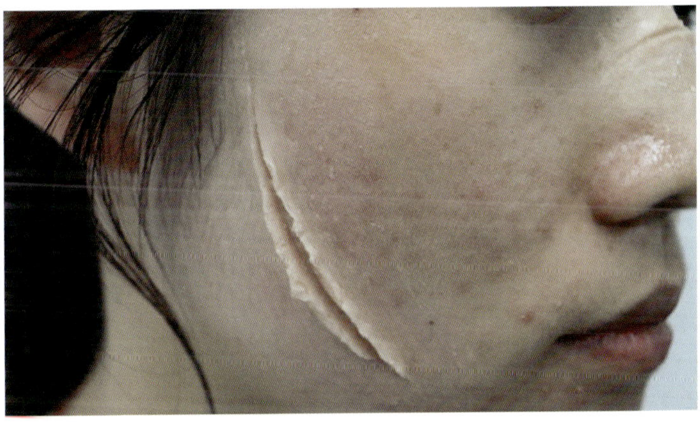

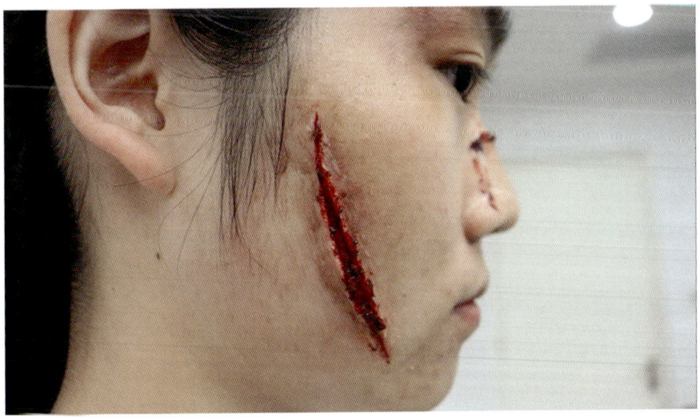

17 级动画 张锦雯

Zhang Jinwen, a student majoring in animation of Grade 2017

媒介文化
Media Culture

学生感言：“在工作坊的若干课程中，媒介文化可以说是最学术的，然而这并不意味着这一门类就是多么的枯燥乏味，相反，它似远实近，在我们生活的众多方面都有着独特而深刻的影响。尤其是在当前环境中，由于媒介的迅速更新与社会开放的不断深入，人们对于媒介文化的认识也更趋于完整全面。”

A student said: “Media culture is arguably the most academic of the courses in the workshop. However, this does not mean that the course is so boring. On the contrary, it seems that it's far away from us, but it's actually close to us. And it has a unique and profound impact on many aspects of our lives. Especially in the current environment, due to the rapid renewal of the media and the deepening opening of the society, people's understanding of media culture is more complete and comprehensive.”

学生感言：“从伊尼斯到麦克卢汉再到波兹曼，老师一步步地带我们更深入地了解媒介文化的发展历程。这种小课堂的形式对我来说是一种新颖的体验。透过这种小型的交互式讲授，我能更进一步地跟紧老师的步伐，同时也能更好地理解老师课堂上的内容。当然，与同学的互动同样是这门课程带给我的全新体验。听课过程中遇到的不懂的问题，可以很方便地与同学近距离探讨。”

A student said: “From Innis to McLuhan and then to Postman, the teacher brings us a deeper understanding of the development process of media culture step by step. This form of small class is a novel experience for me. Through this small interactive lecture, I can follow the teacher's pace further. And at the same time, I can better understand the teaching content from the classroom. Of course, the interaction with my classmates is also a whole new experience that this course brings to me. When I meet some problems that I don’t understand during the course, I can easily discuss with my classmates at close range.”

从青少年角度，看网络短视频

前段时间，有幸接触到一群小学四年级的小孩子，他们活泼、可爱，但每个人却机不离手，整日刷着“抖音”“快手”，捧腹大笑。这里，我想谈谈自己的一点看法，事关娱乐方式，事关短视频。

90年代末的这一代人，小时候娱乐方式虽不如老一辈，却也同样丰富有趣，丢沙包、跳皮筋、支石子、捉迷藏、红绿灯、木头人……课间或放学成为三五游戏的最佳时刻。而10后甚至00后的这一代人，从出生起，便有发达且普遍的电脑及通信技术，互联网带来的不仅是丰富的知识，还有各类令人眼花缭乱的app，从游戏到学术、从文本到视频，衣食住行样样都有，基本涵盖了生活的方方面面。小孩子沉浸在趣味十足的虚拟世界难以自拔，尤其是短视频，更是带给他们前所未有的新鲜体验。这类app把不同地域的人联结在一起，分享有趣的经历，或歌曲，或舞蹈，各类形式一应俱全，使小孩子足不出户便可领略到各类新鲜事物，极大地开阔了他们的眼界。虽然这是以牺牲互动式的课余游戏时间为代价，但总的价值还是值得肯定的。

17级广播电视学 杨丽萍

Viewing Online Short Videos from the Perspective of Teenagers

Some time ago, I was lucky to meet a group of children of fourth grade in primary school. They are lively and cute, but everyone is always holding a cell phone. They use “Tik Tok” and “deft hand” all day long, laughing heartily. Here, I want to talk about my own point of view, about entertainment and short videos.

For people born in the late 1990s, although the forms of entertainment in their childhood were not as good as that of the older generation, they was equally rich and interesting. Beanbag game, rubber band skipping, stone throwing, hide-and-seek, traffic lights, woodman, etc. Class breaks or school breaks are the best time for children to play the games. For both post-2010 and even post-2000 generation, from their birth there are well-developed and widespread computer and communication technologies. Internet brings not only abundant knowledge, but also all kinds of dazzling app. From games to academics, from texts to videos, there are all kinds of clothing, food, shelter and living, which basically cover all aspects of life. Children immerse themselves in the interesting virtual world, and they are difficult to extricate themselves. Especially short videos bring them unprecedented fresh experience. These apps connect people from different regions and share interesting experiences. All kinds of forms are available, including songs and dance, etc. It enables children to appreciate various new things without leaving home, greatly broadening their horizons. Although this is at the expense of interactive after-school game time, the overall value is still worth affirming.

Yang Liping, a student majoring in Radio and Television Science of Grade 2017

《霸王别姬》里的“另一个虞姬”——菊仙

《霸王别姬》是由陈凯歌导演，张国荣、巩俐、张丰毅领衔主演的一部电影。在看《霸王别姬》的时候会有一种戏和生活现实不分的感觉，这种感觉是一种苍白，是一种荒芜的伤感，更是一种无助的绝望。这个世界谁都可以囫囵地、没心没肺地过活，唯独我清醒地、撕裂地、断肠地为我的心之所向付出我的一片真心，即使这种真心被你说成是演戏，即使是被世人所唾弃的“戏子做戏”，我还是把你放在我心中。

电影围绕小楼的两个重要感情人物就是蝶衣和菊仙。蝶衣沉醉于戏，活在戏里，他似乎代表一种相对高洁、不染浮尘的从一而终，就如虞姬一般傲骨。而另一个人物就是菊仙，她是一个妓女。一个妓女的形象似乎是对从一而终的一种极大讽刺，可正是这种讽刺更加使得人伤心。她何尝不是另一个“虞姬”。这两个世人眼里的“假虞姬”，却是真正的虞姬，只是戏里戏外的霸王都是假霸王。这种真假、入戏和现实的强烈冲突使人有一种恍惚、模糊的痛感，这种模糊正是一种无人解、无人怜的痛，世人模糊着他们对真心的记忆，模糊着怜悯，以自己的“真意”和实际为傲，用“戏疯子”践踏着他们所谓的“假意”，一句“为何你不懂”伤了多少可怜之人的心，所以为何我不懂……

如果说蝶衣是一个“明”虞姬，那么菊仙则是一个“暗”虞姬。蝶衣是入戏的，不食人间烟火的；而菊仙则是现实的，染尘濯泥的。可他们最后都决绝地自杀了。这种一明一暗的对比使得影片更加具有意味，也推动了入戏和出世的情节发展。菊仙，一个另类虞姬，一个被生活烟尘摧残的虞姬，她的诀别和虞姬一样是洁白无瑕的。生活的点点滴滴也许是索然无味的粗茶淡饭、繁琐恼人的柴米油盐，也许那些把生活过成戏的人是艺术人生，可是在生活泥潭里摸爬的人何尝不是人生的艺术呢？每一刻每一秒的生活都带着或是浓烈，或是淡云的感情，有有血有肉的悲愤，也有惨淡的绝望，这就是生活。

17 级广播电视学 杨璐

“我这门课程的重点是梳理媒介文化形成和发展的过程，另外我考虑的是，怎样引导同学们在理解媒介文化的基础上，动笔写一些媒介批评方面的文章，也就是文化时评，这也是我们工作坊强调的一种实践。所以我的课程既有理论上的讲解，也有写作方面的内容。”

——授课教师点评

Another "Yu Ji" in the Film *Farewell My Concubine*

Farewell My Concubine is a film directed by CHEN Kaige and starring ZHANG Guorong, GONG Li and ZHANG Fengyi. When watching *Farewell My Concubine*, We feel that the play is inseparable from the reality of life. This feeling is a kind of pallor, a kind of desolate sadness, but also a kind of helpless despair. Everyone in the world can live in a heartless way. I was the only one who gave my heart to what I love. And the sincerity was sober, torn and heartbroken. Even if this kind of sincerity was called acting by you, even if it was called "acting by actors" which was spurned by the world, I still put you in my heart.

In the movie the two important emotional characters around Xiaolou are Dieyi and Juxian. Dieyi was addicted to the play and lived in it. He seems to represent the faithful to his lover unto death, which was a relatively noble and free from floating dust, as proud as Yu Ji. Another character was Juxian, who was a prostitute. The image of a prostitute seems to be a great irony to "the faithful to lover unto death", but it is this irony that makes people sad even more. She was another Yu Ji. These two "false Yu Ji" in the eyes of the world were real Yu Ji. Only the overlords inside and outside the play were all false overlords. The intense conflict between truth and falsehood, drama and reality makes people feel a trance and vague pain. This kind of ambiguity is just a kind of pain that nobody understands and pities. The world blurs their memory of their hearts and their pity. Take pride in their "true meaning" and reality, trample on their so-called "falsehood" with "playful madman". "Why don't you understand" hurts the hearts of so many poor people, so why don't I understand?

If Dieyi was a "bright" Yu Ji, then Juxian was a "dark" Yu Ji. Dieyi was in the theatre and otherworldly. And Juxian was realistic, dusty and muddy. But they all ended up committing suicide. This contrast between light and dark makes the film more meaningful, and also promotes the plot development of entering and leaving the theatre. Juxian was an alternative Yu Ji, destroyed by the smoke and dust of life. Her farewell was as flawless as Yu Ji's. Perhaps every bit of life is tasteless crude tea, light rice, cumbersome and annoying firewood, rice, oil and salt. Maybe those who make life into a play are artistic life, but what about the people who climb in the quagmire of life is not the art of life? Every moment and every second of life is full of strong or light clouds. Life is of flesh and blood, and there is also bleak despair.

Yang Lu, a student majoring in Radio and Television Science of Grade 2017

"The focus of this course is to sort out the formation and development of media culture. In addition, I think about how to guide students to write some articles on media criticism on the basis of understanding media culture, that is, cultural commentary. This is also a practice emphasized by our workshop. So there are both theoretical explanation and writing content in my course." Comments of the teacher."

——Comments of the teacher

领略神奇的 AR 技术

Getting to Know AR

学生感言："在这两天里，成员们加班加点地赶工，我这边程序设计的节点最为重要，所有的想法都在这一环节变成现实，所以编程成为我的一个非常大的挑战。我需要从零开始学习 Unity 引擎和 Vuforia API，然后一步一步将想法变成程序语言。两天时间里，我所写的程序设计上也许并不精美巧妙，但这个经历教给我，只有积累丰富的学习经验，才能一步一步做到更好。"

A student said: "During these two days, the members worked overtime to catch up with the work. The node of my programming is the most important. All ideas come true at this point, so programming is a big challenge for me. I need to learn Unity Engine and Vuforia API from scratch, and then turn ideas into programming languages step by step. In two days, my programming may not be exquisite and ingenious. But this experience teaches me that only by accumulating rich learning experience can we achieve better step by step."

学生感言："这门课程的学习拓宽了我的知识面，使我认识到了更大的世界。由此联想到音乐，应该也是如此，许多新奇的好音乐在源源不断地产生，我们只有不断地去学习新的知识，才能一步步靠近自己最伟大的理想。"

A student said: "The study of this course broadened my knowledge and made me realize the bigger world. Associated with music, it should be the same. Lots of curious and interesting music is constantly emerging. Only by keeping learning new knowledge can we approach our greatest ideals step by step."

"其实这门课程是比较难的，尤其是对非动画专业的同学，而动画专业的学生在建模、程序方面也都没有任何的基础，所以说要完成一个比较复杂的AR应用其实是非常困难的。其实只要每人完成一个作品就可以了，但是17级学生每个组都完成了一个团队作品，他们脑洞大开，特别优秀。"

——授课教师点评

"In fact, this course is rather difficult, especially for students in non-animation majors. And the students majoring in animation have no foundation in modeling and programming. So it is very difficult to complete a more complex AR application. It will be satisfactory if each person completes a work. In fact, each group of students of 2017 Grade has completed a team work. Their mind is greatly enriched, and they are especially excellent."

——Comments of the teacher

17 级广播电视学 司舒舒

Si Shushu, a student majoring in Radio and Television Science of Grade 2017

“虽然这是一个实践性课程，但也不希望大家只盲目地跟着老师做一遍操作，而是能够在思想和理论层面有一些提升。第一天上午是基本原理介绍和实例欣赏，下午做 AR。AR 需要有三维模型，但同学不一定都有三维建模能力，所以这一次采用了一种新的基于照片的三维扫描方式，只要有一个实物，就可以把它立体化做成一个数字模型，在 AR 中展示了。出于这一点考虑，也安排了三维扫描的课程。”

——授课教师点评

17 级动画 李彦卿

Li Yanqing, a student majoring in Animation of Grade 2017

17 级音乐表演 王维斯

Wang Weisi, a student majoring in Music Performance of 2017 Grade

A student said: “Although this is a practical course, I do not want the students to blindly follow me to do the operation. Instead, there are some improvements in the ideological and theoretical level. The introduction of basic principles and the appreciation of examples in the first morning, and AR in the afternoon. AR needs 3D model, but the students do not necessarily have the ability of 3D modeling. So this time a new photo-based three-dimensional scanning method is adopted. As long as there is a physical object, it can be stereotyped into a digital model, which is shown in AR. For this reason, the course about 3D scanning is also arranged.”

—— Comments of the teacher

工作坊日志一页 17 级动画 林芷萱

The page of workshop log Lin Zhixuan, a student majoring in Animation of Grade 2017

韶华 Memories

学生日志

Students' Diaries

夏同学：

“本以为6天会漫长，没想到过得很快，特别是在2天内要完成一个作品、结束一门课程的高速运转模式下。本以为不可能完成的任务，在截止日期近在眼前的压迫下，最后都以令自己满意的成果完成了。由于包含不同专业丰富种类的课程，我们可以打开专业的门，融入一些不一样的血液。不仅打开了一扇门，也打开了一片天地。”

Student Xia,

“I thought six days would be long, but I didn't expect it to go very fast, especially in the high-speed running mode of completing a work and finishing a course in two days. We had thought the tasks were impossible to accomplish, but they were finally finished with satisfactory results under the pressure of the immediate deadline. Because there are many kinds of courses in different majors, we can open the door of different majors and blend in some different blood. It not only opened a door, but also opened a world.”

李同学：

“在这次的工作坊中，我有4天都接触了颜料与绘画。以前我挺排斥画画的，但现在居然有点喜欢了，而且水彩入门书籍和其他水彩颜料已经下单啦！同时我对学院里其他专业的同学有了更多直观的认识，也结交到了一些好朋友。最后汇报会上看到很多优秀的同学，这也激励到了我，我要更加努力去拓展自己的兴趣爱好。”

Student Li,

“In this workshop, I was exposed to paints and paintings for four days. I used to reject painting, but now I kind of like it. And I ordered watercolor introductory books and other watercolor pigments online. At the same time, I have a more intuitive understanding of the students of other majors in the college, and have made some good friends. At the final report summary, I saw many excellent students, which also inspired me. I will try harder to expand my hobbies.”

章同学：

“这次暑假工作坊课程的内容十分丰富，我选择了与专业有相关性的三门课程，通过学习体会了新的艺术形式，并感受到了工艺美术的魅力。美术并不仅局限于画纸与笔，更包含了广阔的材料与逻辑思维。这样的课程形式开拓了学院各专业同学的视野，使我们接触到很多以往难有交集的领域，增添了学习的乐趣。”

Student Zhang,

“The course in this summer workshop is very rich in content. I chose three courses related to my major. Through learning, I got to know the new art form and felt the charm of Arts and crafts. Art is not only limited to drawing paper and pen, but also contains a wide range of materials and logical thinking. This form of curriculum opens up the vision of students of all majors in the college, makes us come into contact with a lot of areas that we hardly had oppotunities to connect in the past, and adds to the fun of learning.”

吉同学：

“每一次新的体验、每一次机会、每一次探讨、每一次学习，短短几天时间的实践周挖掘出了我更多的可能性与潜力。通过工作坊，我认识了许多非广编专业的同学；在合作、交流的过程中，也发现不同专业同学的闪光点。新闻的同学有想法、有主见；动画的同学总有奇思妙想；音表的同学音乐素养令我十分羡慕……我认为，跨专业、跨领域的人才是未来的社会所需求的，若还有机会，我会尝试去学习更多领域的知识，提升自己的艺术素养。”

Student Ji,

“Every new experience, every opportunity, every discussion, every learning. In just a few days of practice week, it taps out more possibilities and potentials for me. Through the workshop, I know many students who do not major in Radio and Television Editor. In the process of cooperation and communication, I also found the shining points of different professional classmates. The students who major in Journalism have ideas and opinions, those who major in Animation always have fantastic ideas, and the musicianship of those students who major in Music Performance makes me envy them very much. In my opinion, cross-disciplinary talents are the needs of the future society. If I have the chance, I will try to learn the knowledge about more fields, and improve my artistic accomplishment.”

王同学：

“六天的工作坊很快结束了，说实话，还有些许意犹未尽。在这六天的课程中，我接触到了柳老师讲述的前卫的AR技术；领略了拥有瞬间之美的特效摄影，以及拼了命去拍素材、剪视频的延时摄影。不仅在自己的专业方面有所收获，也学到了更多跨学科的知识，更学会了一些软件的应用。”

Student Wang,

“The six-day workshop was soon over. To tell you the truth, it leaves me wanting more. During the six-day course, I was exposed to the avant-garde AR technology described by Mr. LIU, appreciated special effects photography with instant beauty, and experienced the time-lapse photography of shooting materials and cutting videos desperately. I not only gained in my profession, but also learned more interdisciplinary knowledge and some software applications.”

张同学：

“在我们学校中，就数传院的小学期最有意思。在我看来，小学期课程的共同点在于把生活中‘高大上’的技术带到我们的身边。我们可以在光影中感受火、水与生命的碰撞；在化妆的一笔一画中感受高超的技艺；用计算机创造、策划、设计版式……”

Student Zhang,

“In our school, the elementary semester in College of Arts & Media is the most interesting. In my opinion, the common point of the curriculum in the elementary semester is to bring the splendid technology into our lives. We can feel the collision of fire, water and life in light and shadow. We can feel superb skill in every painting of makeup. We can create, plan and design format with the computer.”

王同学：

“除了收获知识，在工作坊课程中，也结识了更多的伙伴。大家欢声笑语，互相帮助解决问题，让我们在繁忙的学习之余多了一些欢乐。工作坊让我学会了很多，我感到今后的专业课学习不会很轻松，这也是给自己的一个提醒，要利用假期，合理分配时间。”

Student Wang,

“In addition to harvesting knowledge, more partners have been made in the courses of workshop. Everyone laughs and helps each other to solve problems, which brings fun to our busy study. The workshop taught me a lot. I came to realize it won't be easy for me to learn professional courses in the future. This was also a reminder to myself that I should make use of my holidays and allocate my time reasonably.”

孙同学：

“实践周为我们提供了一些很有趣的课程，也给了我们许多选择的余地。在这里我学到了很多，也交到了不同专业的新朋友。惟新馆建筑很有艺术气息，这里学习氛围浓厚，也不乏娱乐的空间。希望我能够学以致用，用这几天所学到的东西为接下来的三年做好铺垫。能在惟新馆里学习广播电视编导的专业知识真的很让人开心。”

Student Sun,

“Practice Week provides us with some interesting courses, as well as a lot of choices. I learned a lot here and made new friends from different majors. The architecture of Weixin Building is very artistic. There is a strong learning atmosphere, and there is no lack of entertainment space. I hope I can apply what I have learned in these days to pave the way for the next three years. It' really enjoyable to learn the professional knowledge of Radio and Television Editor in Weixin Building.”

王同学：

“在学习结束后的暑假，我决定安排一系列‘见世面’活动，比如观摩大师课和音乐会，去网上翻阅音乐界的各类新奇的新闻，以及增加在琴房练习的时间。我还想要增加课外知识的学习，比如人工智能机器的编程，希望能够赶上人工智能的潮流，以此辅助我的音乐学习之路。”

Student Wang,

“In the summer vacation after the workshop, I decide to arrange a series of activities of 'See the World'. For example, watching master classes and concerts, reading all kinds of news in the music industry online, and increasing the time of practice in the piano room. I also want to increase learning extra-curricular knowledge, such as artificial intelligence machine programming, hoping to catch up with the trend of artificial intelligence, in order to assist my path of learning music.”

丁同学：

亲爱的工作坊
愿你能一直一直带领着艺传人
见天地
见众生
我会更好地生
更好地活
更好地生活
我们的故事
未完待续

Student Ding,

Dear Workshop
I hope you can always lead the students of College of Arts & Media
To see the world
To see all living beings
I will live a better life.
Our story is not finished yet.

工作坊日志一页 17 级动画 林芷萱

The page of workshop log Lin Zhixuan, a student majoring in Animation of Grade 2017

问卷 Questionnaire

前言

Preface

本次问卷调查对象是同济大学艺术与传媒学院 2018 年度暑期实践工作坊参与人员，主要包括本学院 2017 级广播电视学、广告学、广播电视编导、动画、影视表演、音乐表演等六个专业的本科生，意在了解被调查者对于本次暑期实践工作坊相关工作安排的意见和评价，作为后续工作的改进参考。问卷于 2018 年 7 月 24 日下午正式通过问卷星平台进行发放，最终回收有效问卷 155 份。

This questionnaire report is based on the questionnaire for 2018 summer workshop of the college of arts and media. It is intended to get the advice and feedbacks on the arrangement of the summer workshop, which will be used as the reference to improve the follow-up work. This survey mainly aimed at the participants of the workshop mentioned above. They are the undergraduate students of Grade 2017 from the following six majors: broadcast & TV journalism, advertising, broadcast & TV directing, animation, performance and music performance. The questionnaire was formally distributed on the afternoon of July 24, 2018 through the questionnaire platform named as 'Wenjuanxing'. Finally 155 valid questionnaires were collected. Now the information of the questionnaire survey is summarized to form the report.

该评测分数的设置参考李克特“五点”量表，将不同程度的评价运用不同强度的描述语加以呈现，而李克特量表中是以“无所谓”这一选项为 0 基点，各向上下两个程度进行延伸，本问卷则与之不同，以基本满意为基点。

The evaluation scores are set up according to the Likert's ‘five-point’ scale, in which different levels of evaluation correspond to the description of different intensity. The difference is that in the Likert scale the ‘indifferent’ option is 0 points and the score extends to two ends. However the questionnaire is based on basic satisfaction.

问卷基本信息

The Basic Information of the Questionnaire

一、问卷问题设置

The set of the questions

本次问卷从课程调剂安排、课程类型的偏向、课程安排与内容满意程度、自我能力提升，以及暑期实践工作坊整体工作安排等多个方面共设计了 16 道题目，其中 14 道为单选题，要求被调查者从列出的选项中只选出一项；一道为弹性多选题，要求被调查者从列出的选项中选出一项或者多项；一道为填空题，主要收集被调查者对本次暑期实践工作坊的其他意见，为后续改进提供直接有效的参考。

The questionnaire includes 16 questions on the arrangement of course adjustment, the bias of course type, course arrangements and the degree of satisfaction, self-improvement, and the overall arrangement of the summer workshop. 14 questions are multiple choices, and the interviewees should choose only one from the given options. One question is a flexible multiple choice, namely the interviewees are required to choose one or more. The rest requires the interviewees to fill in the blank spaces, which mainly aims to collect other opinions on the summer workshop, to provide direct and effective reference for subsequent improvement.

1. 课程调剂安排

The arrangement of course adjustment

本次选课主要依据学生填报志愿的先后时间进行课程资源分配，因为部分课程容量有限，未选上该课程的学生该项志愿无效，将会面临课程调剂的问题。这一部分的问卷，期望了解在不得不进行调剂的情况下，学生是否有被调剂、对调剂结果的满意程度等，便于日后完善选课安排，以尽最大能力满足学生对课程的需求，发现其兴趣所在。

This course selection is mainly based on the priority time of students' filling in and submitting their wishes. Because of the limited curriculum capacity, the wish of the students who fail to select the course is invalid, and these students face the problem of course adjustment. By this part of the questionnaire, we hope to know whether the students are reassigned, and their satisfaction degree with the result of adjustment, under the circumstances that the adjustments have to be made. It is convenient to improve the course selection arrangement in future so as to meet the students' demands, and find out their interests.

2. 课程类型的偏向

The bias of course type

暑期实践工作坊主要课程安排偏向于实践性，同时也积极提倡通过丰富多样的课程类型让学生进行跨学科、跨领域的学习与合作，所以在具体的课程设置上分为四个类型：媒体基础素养类课程（如音乐、台词表演等）、媒体专业技术类课程（如摄影、摄像等）、实践拓展类课程（如木刻、树脂画、特效化妆等）、技术前沿类课程（如AR技术等）。在充分保证课程类型多样化的前提之下，问卷意在了解学生在课程类型上的偏好，以在之后的课程设置中更好地激发学生的学习兴趣。

Summer Practice Workshop mainly focuses on practicality, and actively advocates interdisciplinary learning and cooperation among students through a variety of curriculum types. Therefore, these lessons are divided into four types: basic media literacy lessons (e.g. music, lines and dialogues performance, etc.), media professional technique lessons (e.g. photography, camera shooting, etc.), practical extension lessons (e.g. woodcut, 3D resin painting, special effects make-up for film and TV works, etc.), technological frontier lessons (e.g. AR technology, etc.). On the premise of fully guaranteeing the variety of course types, this questionnaire is designed to understand the students' preference on the course type, in order to better stimulate students' interest in learning In the following curriculum settings.

3. 课程安排及内容

Course arrangement and content satisfaction

问卷内容意在探究学生对课程安排包括上课时间安排的满意程度，以优化暑期实践工作坊的课程安排。同时该方面还涉及安排的时间等方面，方便之后就暑期实践工作坊的课程时间进行调整，提高同学们的满意度。

The survey intends to explore the students' satisfaction with the course arrangement, including class time arrangement, in order to optimize the course arrangement of summer workshop. Meanwhile it also involves the arrangement of time and so on. It’s helpful to adjust the time arrangement of summer workshop, and improve the students’ satisfaction degree.

4. 自我能力提升

Self-ability promotion

开展暑期实践工作坊的主旨在于提升学生的个人能力、拓展其知识视野。教学成效是检验教学安排合理与否的量度。这一部分的问卷，主要通过了解学生个人在自我提高和成果制作上的主观感知，探究教学的实际收效。

The purpose of the summer workshop is to enhance students' personal ability, and broaden their knowledge and horizon. Teaching effectiveness is a measure of whether teaching arrangement is reasonable or not. This part of the questionnaire explores the actual teaching effect mainly by understanding students' subjective perception on their self-improvement and work production.

5. 总体评价

Overall evaluation

这一部分主要设置三道题目，以了解学生对暑期实践工作坊内容的总体评价和反馈意见。

In terms of overall evaluation, mainly 3 questions are set to understand the overall evaluation and feedback of the students on the contents of the summer workshop.

二、问题选项设置

Question Options Settings

本问卷主要包括单独设项类题目和评价类题目两种。其中单独设项类题目的选项尽可能涵盖学生所能想到答案的各种类型；评价类题目在选项设置上则主要分为5档，如下表所示：

The questions in this questionnaire are mainly divided into individual option and evaluation, in which the individual option questions provide as many types of answers as possible that students can think of. While the options of the evaluation questions are mainly divided into 5 levels, as shown in the following table:

设置等级 *Level*	设置内容 *Content*
1	非常符合 / 非常满意 Very reasonable/Very satisfied
2	较为符合 / 较为满意 Fairly reasonable/Fairly satisfied
3	基本符合 / 基本满意 Basically reasonable/ Basically satisfied
4	不符合 / 不满意 Fairly unreasonable/ Fairly dissatisfied
5	很不符合 / 很不满意 Very unreasonable/Very dissatisfied

三、问卷结果概览
Result Overview

第 1 题 您对此次的选课规则设置是否满意？［单选题］

QUESTION 1 Are you satisfied with the elective rules?[single-choice question]

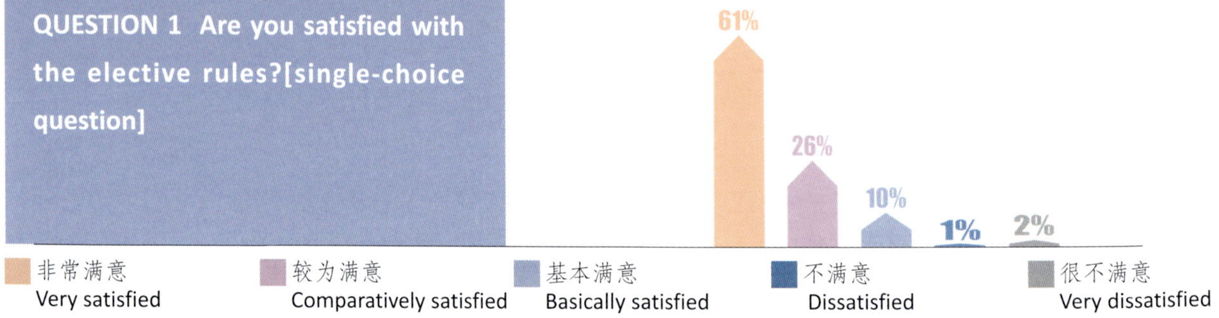

第 2 题 您对此次的选课工作安排（选课时间、选课平台、选课告知工作等）是否满意？［单选题］

QUESTION 2 Are you satisfied with the elective arrangement? (Including selection schedule, selection platform, and selection notification, etc.) [single-choice question]

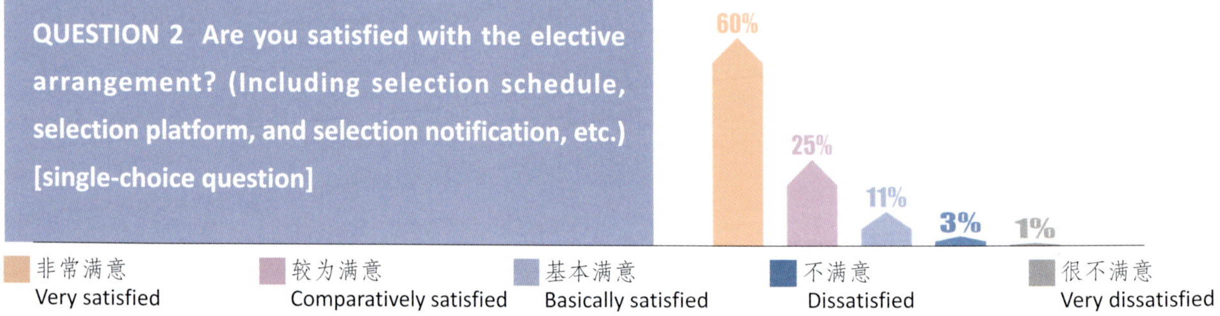

第 3 题 您对此次的课程安排是否满意？［单选题］

QUESTION 3 Are you satisfied with the course arrangement?[single-choice question]

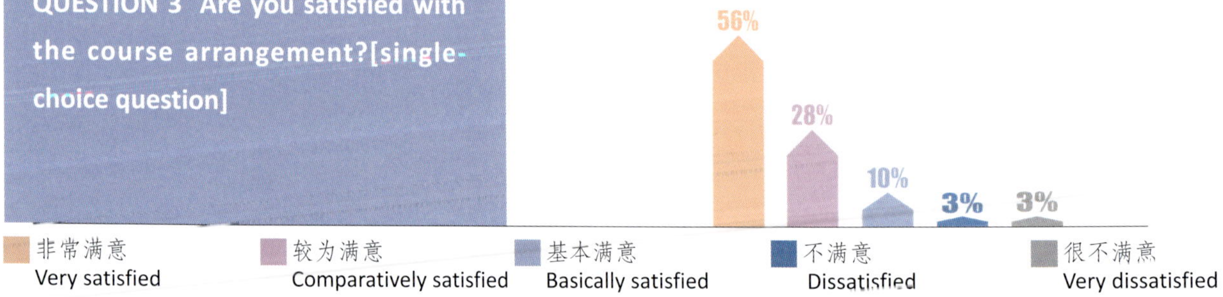

第 4 题　您最终的课程安排是否符合您的选课预期？［单选题］

QUESTION 4　Is your final course arrangement consistent with your expectation? [single-choice question]

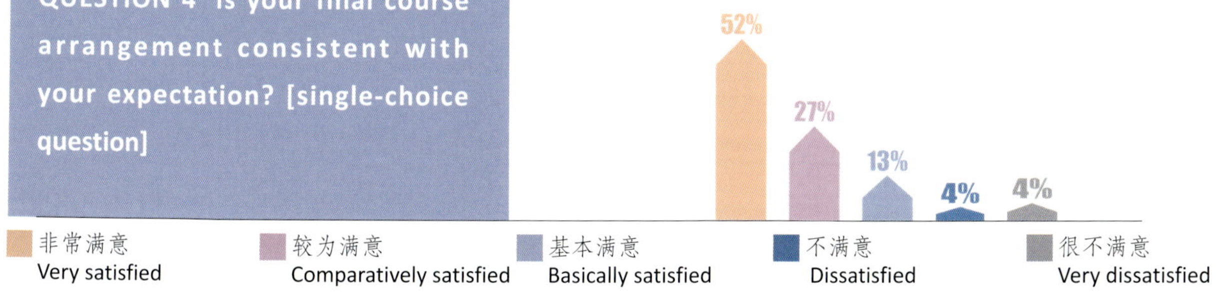

第 5 题　在这期暑期实践工作坊中，您最满意的课程是哪一门？［单选题］

QUESTION 5　Which course are you most satisfied with in the summer workshop? [single-choice question]

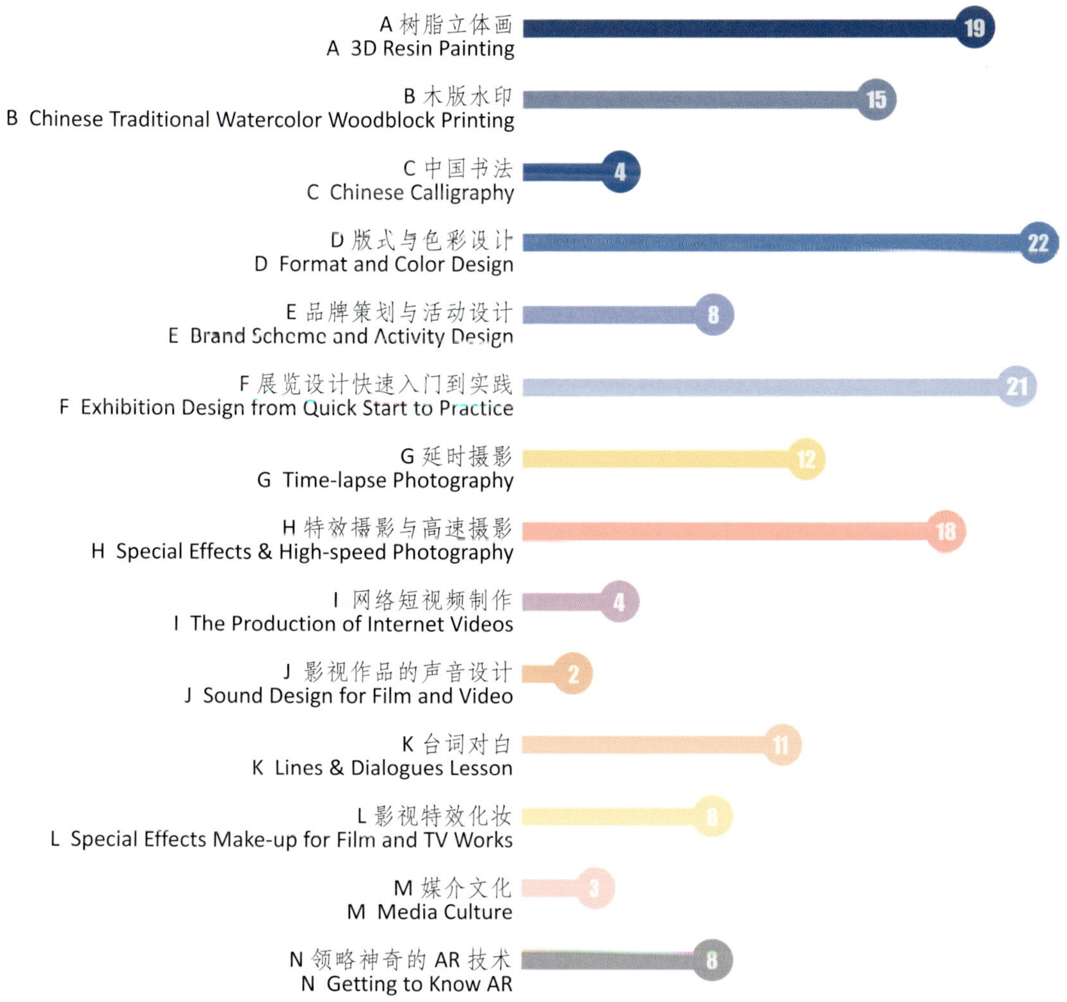

第 6 题　您对课程教师的教学安排是否满意？［单选题］

QUESTION 6　Are you satisfied with the teachers' arrangements for the lessons?[single-choice question]

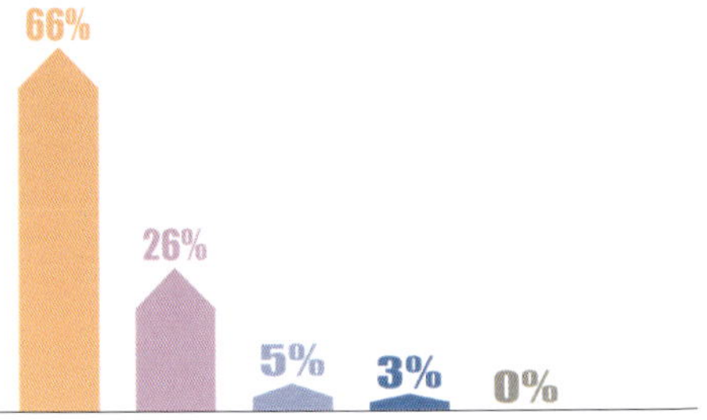

非常满意 Very satisfied　较为满意 Comparatively satisfied　基本满意 Basically satisfied　不满意 Dissatisfied　很不满意 Very dissatisfied

第 7 题　您对课程实际的教学内容是否满意？［单选题］

QUESTION 7　Are you satisfied with the actual teaching content?[single-choice question]

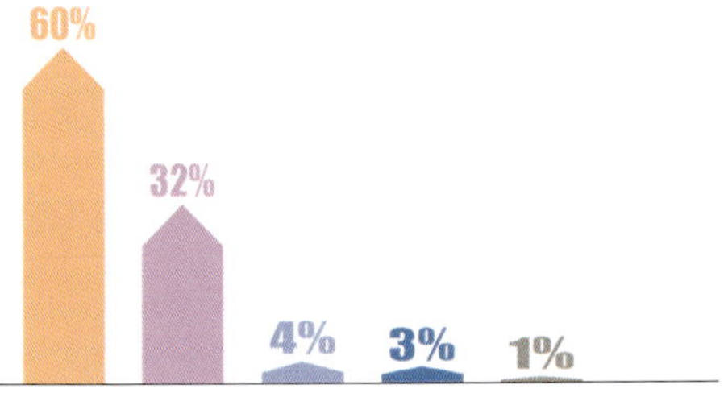

非常满意 Very satisfied　较为满意 Comparatively satisfied　基本满意 Basically satisfied　不满意 Dissatisfied　很不满意 Very dissatisfied

第 8 题　您对最终要求提交的课程成果是否满意？［单选题］

QUESTION 8　Are you satisfied with your final works?[single-choice question]

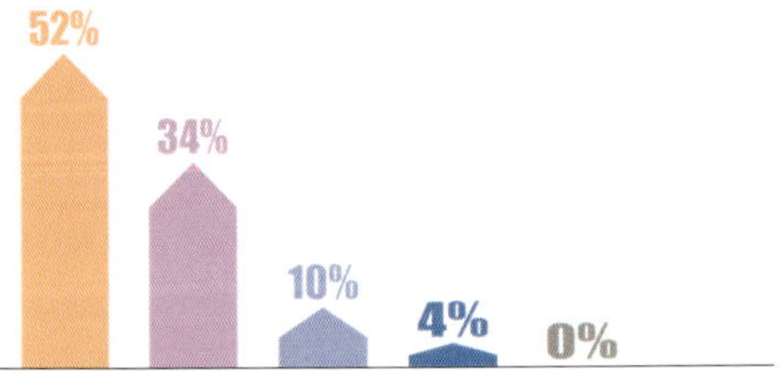

非常满意 Very satisfied　较为满意 Comparatively satisfied　基本满意 Basically satisfied　不满意 Dissatisfied　很不满意 Very dissatisfied

第 9 题 您对自我的课程表现是否满意？［单选题］

QUESTION 9 Are you satisfied with your performance during the lessons?[single-choice question]

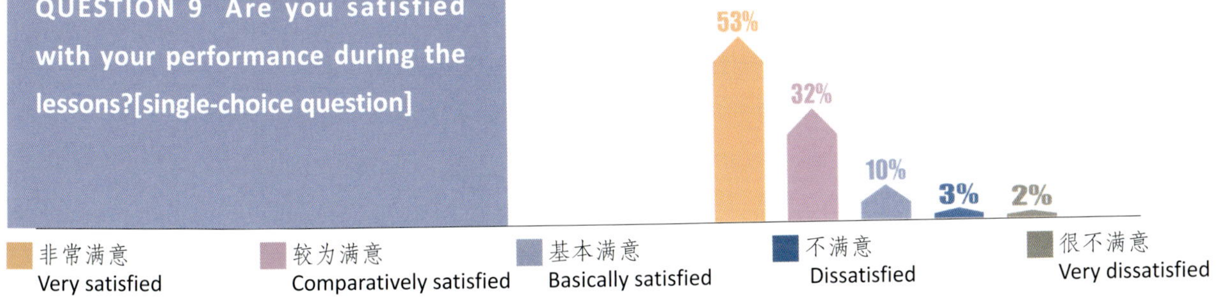

第 10 题 通过本次暑期课程，您觉得在哪些方面获得了提高？［多选题］

QUESTION 10 What abilities do you think have been improved during the course?[multiple-choice question]

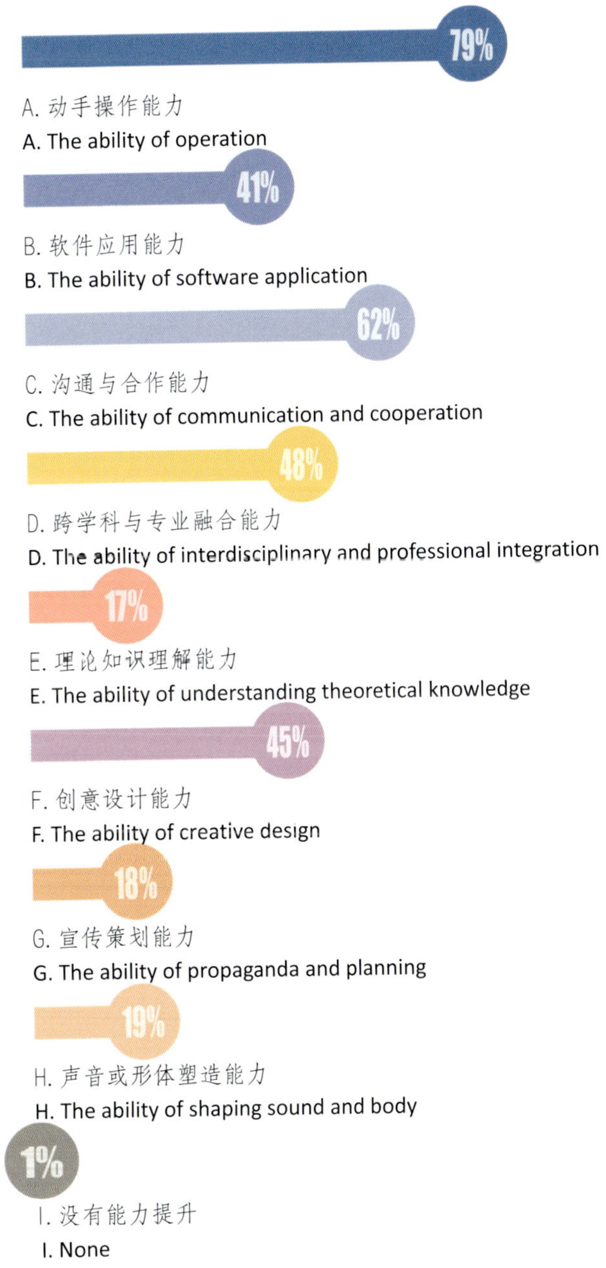

第 11 题 您觉得通过本次实践工作坊学习，您的各方面能力有所提升吗？［单选题］

QUESTION 11 Do you think your abilities have been improved during the workshop?[single-choice question]

第 12 题 请您对本次暑期实践周课程教学进行评价。［单选题］

QUESTION 12 Please comment on the teaching of the workshop. [single-choice question]

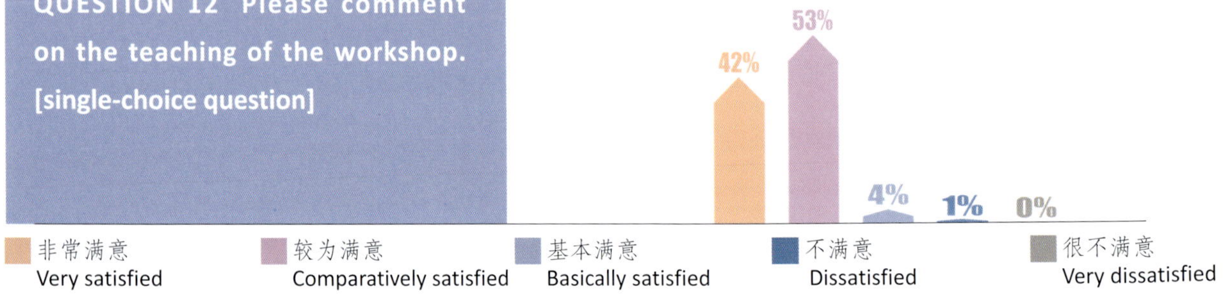

第 13 题 请您对本次暑期实践周的整体工作进行评价。［单选题］

QUESTION 13 Please give your overall evaluation of the workshop. [single-choice question]

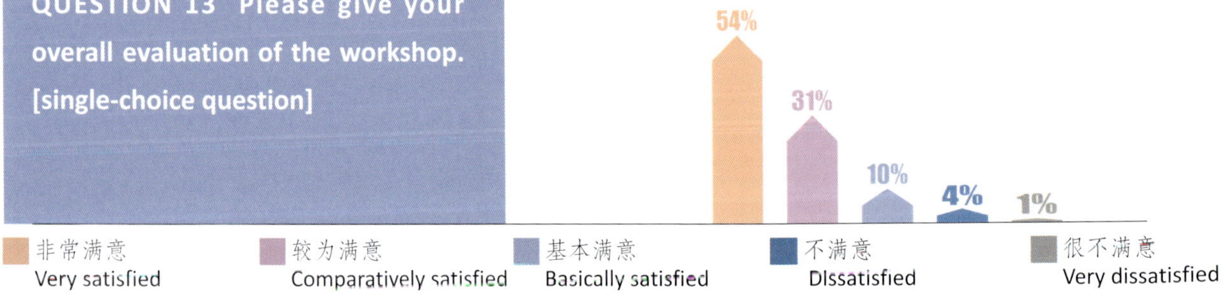

第 14 题 您对自己在暑期实践周的表现如何评价？［单选题］

QUESTION 14 How do you evaluate your performance during the course?[single-choice question]

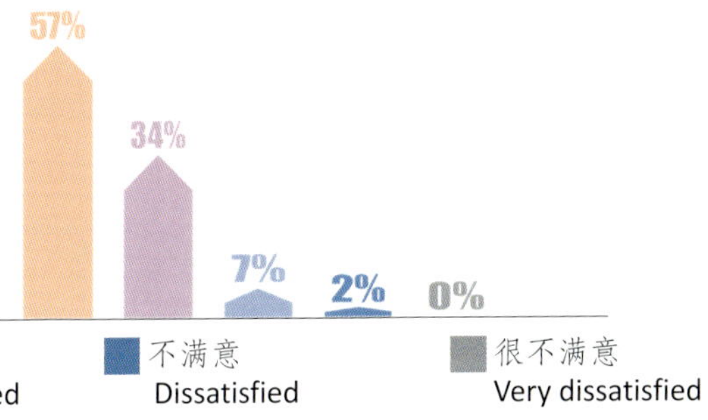

第 15 题 您认为暑期实践周还有什么需要改进的地方？ _______［填空题］

QUESTION 15 What do you think needs to be improved in summer workshop? _______ [completion question]

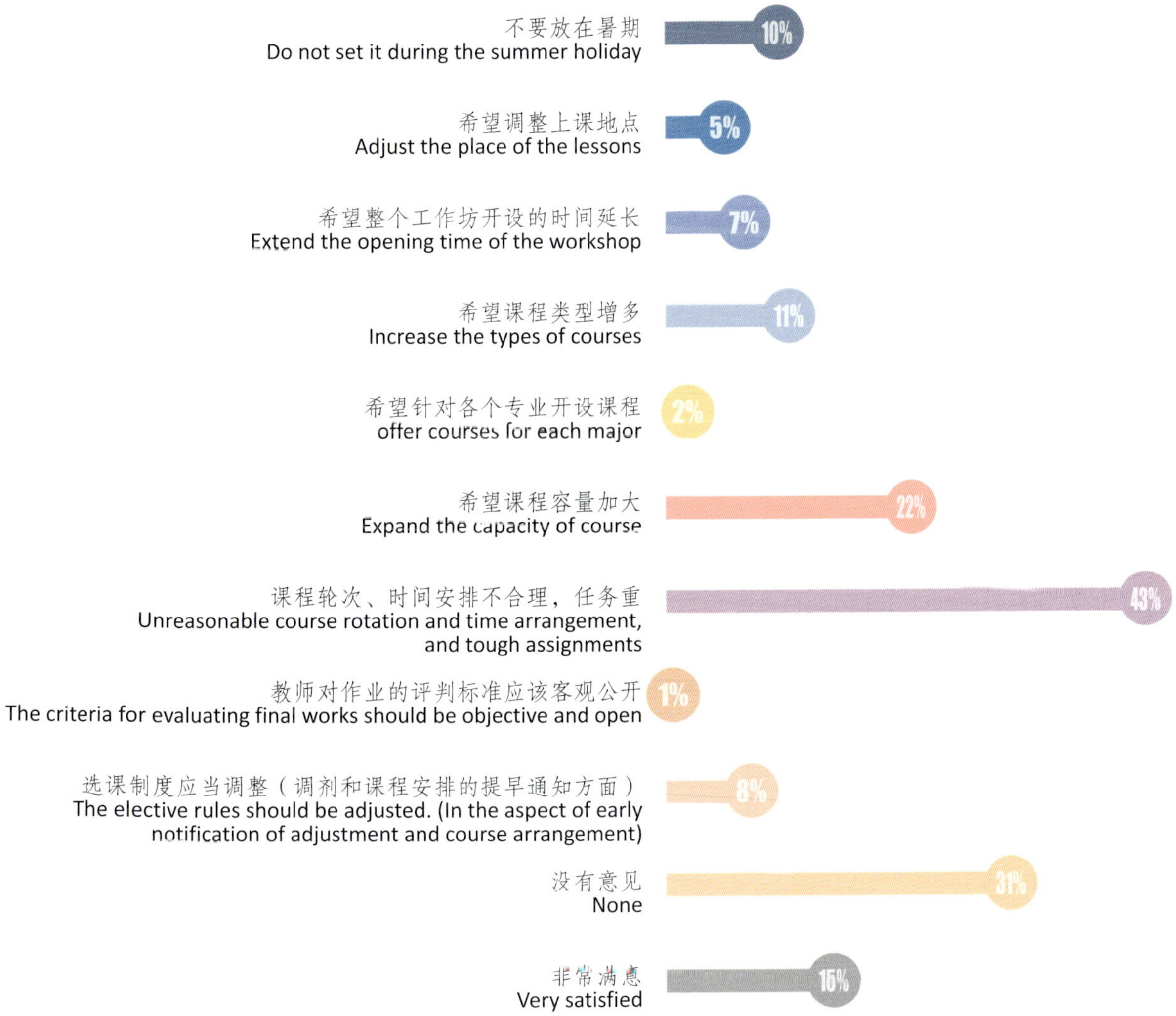

问卷整体分析

Overall Analysis of Questionnaires

在工作坊课程不断的改进与丰富之下，学生们在暑期实践工作坊中的参与度和收获度都有大幅度提升。在课程安排与规则设置上，前期选课强调在最大化满足学生兴趣的前提下，兼具公平公正公开的原则。调查结果显示只有3%的学生选择了不满意。

The courses of workshops are constantly improving and enriching. Students' participation and harvest in summer practice workshops have been greatly improved. In terms of curriculum arrangement and rule setting, the course selection of early stage emphasizes the principle of fairness, justice and openness on the premise of meeting students' interests to the greatest extent. The results of survey show that only 3% of the students are unsatisfied with the setting of course selection rules.

在课程类型设置上，基础素养、媒体技术、实践拓展三种类别的课程深受学生们的喜爱，这也表明密集实践性课程的设置满足了大多数学生对暑期实践工作坊的期待。就单门课程而言，学生最满意的三门课程分别是饶丹云老师开设的“台词对白”、梅琼林老师开设的“中国书法”和廖莎莎老师开设的“树脂立体画”。80%的学生认为通过此次工作坊动手操作能力得到了提高，45%的学生认为沟通能力得到了提升，40%的学生认为提高了创意设计能力。

Regarding the course type, basic literacy lessons, media technique lessons and practical extension lessons are more preferred, which also shows that the setting of intensive practical courses meets most students' expectation of the workshop. And for each lesson, three most favored lessons are Lines & Dialogues lesson by Rao danyun, Chinese calligraphy by Mei Qionglin, and 3D resin painting by Liao Shasha. 80% of the students feel that their hands-on operation ability is improved, which is ranked first. And the second and the third ranking are the ability of communication and creative design, which account for 45% and 40% respectively.

从中可以看到，融媒体暑期实践工作坊通过三门跨专业课程，实现在理论上的跨界学习、实践上的跨界交融、项目上的跨界合作，课程宗旨得到了充分的体现。此外，融媒体暑期实践工作坊也推动了学生在团队合作方面的提升，培养学生的交流能力、合作能力与解决问题的能力。同时，学生的创意想法借助课程作品有机会在更广阔、更前沿的平台上得到展示，让学生有更多的创作动力。

It can be seen from this that the integration media summer practice workshop realizes cross-border learning in theory, cross-border blending in practice and cross-border cooperation in projects through three cross-border courses. The purpose of the course has been fully reflected. In addition, the integration media summer practice workshop also promotes the improvement of students' team cooperation, and cultivates students' abilities of communication, cooperation and problem-solving. At the same time, students' creative ideas have the opportunity to be displayed on a broader and more cutting-edge platform with the help of course works, so as to stimulate more motivation of students.

从本次工作坊课程教学质量来看，42％的学生认为超过预期，53％的学生认为达到预期。但同时工作坊需要改进的地方，也收到学生们关于课程轮次、时间安排不合理、任务过重等的反馈。未来再次开设工作坊时，将在课后作业布置量上考虑到与之后不同课程之间的衔接问题，以优化课后作业作品提交的时间节点，尽量避免学生连续高强度学习的情况出现，给予学生充足的时间消化知识、提升技能。

On the teaching quality of the workshop courses, 42% of the students think that it's beyond their expectation, and 53% of the students think it meets their expectation. But at the same time, the workshop needs to be improved in some aspects. We also get some feedbacks about unreasonable curriculum rotation and schedule, and some of the study missions are kind of heavy. When the workshop is opened again in the future, we will consider the connection with different courses in the amount of homework after class. We will optimize the deadline for the submission of homework to avoid continuous and high-intensity learning. We will give students enough time to digest knowledge and improve their skills.

在自我课程表现方面，53％的学生给自己打了非常满意的高分，32％的学生较为满意，这一结果也与学生对自己课程成果的满意度相呼应。由此不仅可以看出本期融媒体暑期实践工作坊在工作安排、课程设置等内容上基本实现了最初的目标和期待，也感受到了学生的的认可与肯定，三门课程学习投入的时间精力都是有价值、有收获的。

In terms of self-curriculum performance, 53% of the students are very satisfied with themselves, 32% of the students feel comparatively satisfied, and this result is in accordance with their satisfaction of the final works of their lessons. As a result, the summer practice workshop of media integration has not only achieved the original goal and expectations on the work arrangement and curriculum setting, but also approved and affirmed by students. The time and energy invested in the three courses are valuable and fruitful.

问卷中我们也收集到了可供工作坊进一步改善的参考内容，一是课程设计方面，可适当增加课程的类型，同时针对课程的难易程度来调整课程课时、优化课程容量等。二是在前期准备时，应尽早给出各课程的准确上课时间，让同学们能自我安排；课程轮次能够均匀分配，给予学生充分的时间完成任务；兼顾满足兴趣和提升技能两方面，提升学生的各项能力并激发出学生更多的创造力。

In the questionnaire, we have also collected references for further improvement of the workshop. One is about curriculum design, it is suggested that we could appropriately increase the types of courses, adjust the course hours according to the difficulty of the course, and optimize the setting of the capacity. The other is in the early preparation. We should give the exact class time of each course as early as possible so that students can arrange themselves earlier. The course rounds could be evenly distributed, giving students sufficient time to complete tasks. We will also give consideration to both meeting students' interests and improving their skills, enhance students' abilities and stimulate their creativity.

工作坊日志一页 17 级动画 唐文萱

The page of workshop log Tang Wenxun, a student majoring in Animation of Grade 2017

后记 Postscript

致谢

Acknowledgements

首先，感谢每一位付出了心血的模块课程教师
没有你们加班加点的辛勤付出就没有异彩纷呈的模块课程

其次，感谢所有参与工作坊课程的 2017 级本科生
你们的积极努力不仅为实践课程画上了浓墨重彩的一笔，更鼓舞了教师与课程组的信心

感谢金云水、徐逸君、刘芸老师对本次工作坊进行缜密规划
并自始至终工作在课程一线，确保活动的顺利进行

感谢笔克展览服务有限公司对本次工作坊课程的鼎力支持
并安排汪源总监亲自授课

感谢李睿书记为工作坊课程住宿、选课问题的落实前后奔走

感谢王胜、陈慧玲、丑科钰、鲍雨迪、蒋辰雨同学
为整个课程东奔西走，用镜头记录下工作坊的点点滴滴

感谢刘芸老师和甘露顺、杨晨青、杨鉴琳、黄俊仪同学
为保障此次工作坊的选课与排课的落实、材料与场地的准备、问卷的采访调查而尽心尽力

感谢李夏老师和甘露顺、刘悦同学为工作坊的宣传与推广夜以继日地精心打造

感谢徐逸君老师为工作坊课程设计了引人瞩目的宣传资料
感谢刘术一老师、蔡蕾同学为工作坊出版内容提供高水平翻译

感谢朱隆喜、徐逸君、刘芸老师为课程提供场地与设备方面的支持

感谢徐晓东老师为课程落实接送班车

最后，再次感谢每一位上面提到或者不慎遗漏的为工作坊课程做出贡献的人！

2018 暑期实验与实践工作坊课程组
同济大学艺术与传媒学院

Firstly, we would like to thank all teachers who open these fantastic courses.
Without your delicate contributions, these courses would not be so successful.

We also must thank all undergraduate students of grade 2017. Your energetic participation in these courses is of vital importance, giving more confidence to teachers and organization committee.

We would also like to thank Mr. Jin Yunshui, Miss Xu Yijun and Miss Liu Yun who made a detailed plan and engaged in all courses to make sure every section work well.

We are indebted to Pico Exhibition Company for providing great support
and President Director Wang Yuan of Pico who gave lessons personally.

Thanks to Secretary Mr. Li Rui for helping students choose courses and arranging their accommodation.

Thanks to Wang Sheng, Cheng Huilin, Chou Keyu, Bao Yudi, Jiang Chenyu
who took videos during the process.

Thanks to Miss Liu Yun, Gan Lushun, Yang Chenqing, Yang Jianlin, Huang Junyi for their dedication in course arrangement, preparation for teaching materials and classrooms, and questionnaire.

Thanks to Mrs. Li Xia, Gan Lushun, Liu Yue for promoting and reporting the workshop on internet.

Thanks to Miss Xu Yijun for designing all kinds of promotional products; to Liu Shuyi and Cai Lei for providing high-quality translation for the Workshops.

Thanks to Zhu Longxi, Xu Yijun, Liu Yun for offering support of equipment and space; to Xu Xiaodong for ferrying students.

Lastly, thanks again to the above-mentioned people and those unmentioned ones, who made contributions to the workshop!

Organizing Committee of the 2018 Experiment and Practice Workshop
College of Arts and Media, Tongji University

全体参与人员名单

List of All Participants

廖莎莎	金云水	丑科钰	蒋原伦	朱哲淇	张轶婧
费 俞	徐逸君	鲍雨迪	柳喆俊	江雪瑶	陈 好
梅琼林	董 华	蒋辰雨	周 丽	王芳天	秦敬鸿
由 芳	刘 芸	袁璐瑶	朱贤文	唐 颖	朴壮彬
王建民	刘木一	杨超凡	沈 诗	王蓓妮	李美霖
汪 源	蔡 蕾	贾文雅	吕思诺	黄 菁	徐英男
方红峰	杨晨青	吴 荣	徐珂宇	张添羿	袁玉瑶
薛 航	黄俊仪	吴 琼	孙世鹏	尹梓阳	刘 婷
任玲玲	杨鉴琳	熊 欣	李 颖	张铭轩	萨米娜
万 方	许 奕	金 婧	陈媛仪	林采薇	禹常晶
饶丹云	王 胜	顾 婧	郭 霆	黄嘉欣	郑相麒
房巧玉	陈慧玲	陈彦百	丁佳妍	朱天昀	范斯晶
钟梦婷	张超楠	李泽茜	史寅颖	徐刘莹	朴容奭
秦一琪	张昕	李秀聪	张天鹤	王兆阳	王佳沛
王一涵	吴华静	章一诺	王艺颖	唐与颉	任益明
孙铭锌	张曦	许屹菲	李辉雪	刘宣奕	贾雨翔
张信真	苏婷	陶以诺	刘泓妤	佟 心	宁 静

尹雨凤	张天羽	王慧珺	王一丞	王欣宇	于琳芸
郑芷仪	叶富艺	薛佳颖	杨　洋	宋怡文	薛　亮
杨家程	艾文杰	梁慧妍	钟梓洋	陈家璐	李嘉欣
杨丽萍	李云婷	王维斯	王心宁	章傲涵	王　宇
张宇昭	谷文宁	陈嘉颖	章　燕	李彦卿	吉文莉
朱硕琳	刘　鑫	徐舟爽	谢钰洁	金　毅	裴宴宁
杨　苏	刘　杨	李媛媛	楼可静	李欣然	何熠凌
王修平	曾菀婷	王　晴	卢　玥	周星宇	孙景怡
庞猗菁	卜丹亚	肖　婵	楼纯涵	沈佳玮	高　畅
莫周婷	印　名	周鑫鑫	陈佳音	张怀尹	张越淇
许芯蕾	徐　菁	杨采妮	李孟真	张锦雯	林昕宜
王翊萌	何紫涵	覃　朗	孙小琳	卫　敏	张必青
周家旭	张紫凌	周凌越	张　一	陈舒婷	彭　肖
魏琳迪	郑茜琳	钱成虹	丁熙桐	唐泽雨	贾雯晔
林芷萱	陈　爽	司舒舒	张兴泰	马　蓉	陈涵睿
章轶文	夏仕欣	唐文蕈	陈舒舒	郑仲燕	蔡筱君
王　叶	杨　璐	孙　盼	林　好	李嘉祺	王奕博

签名版

Signature Board

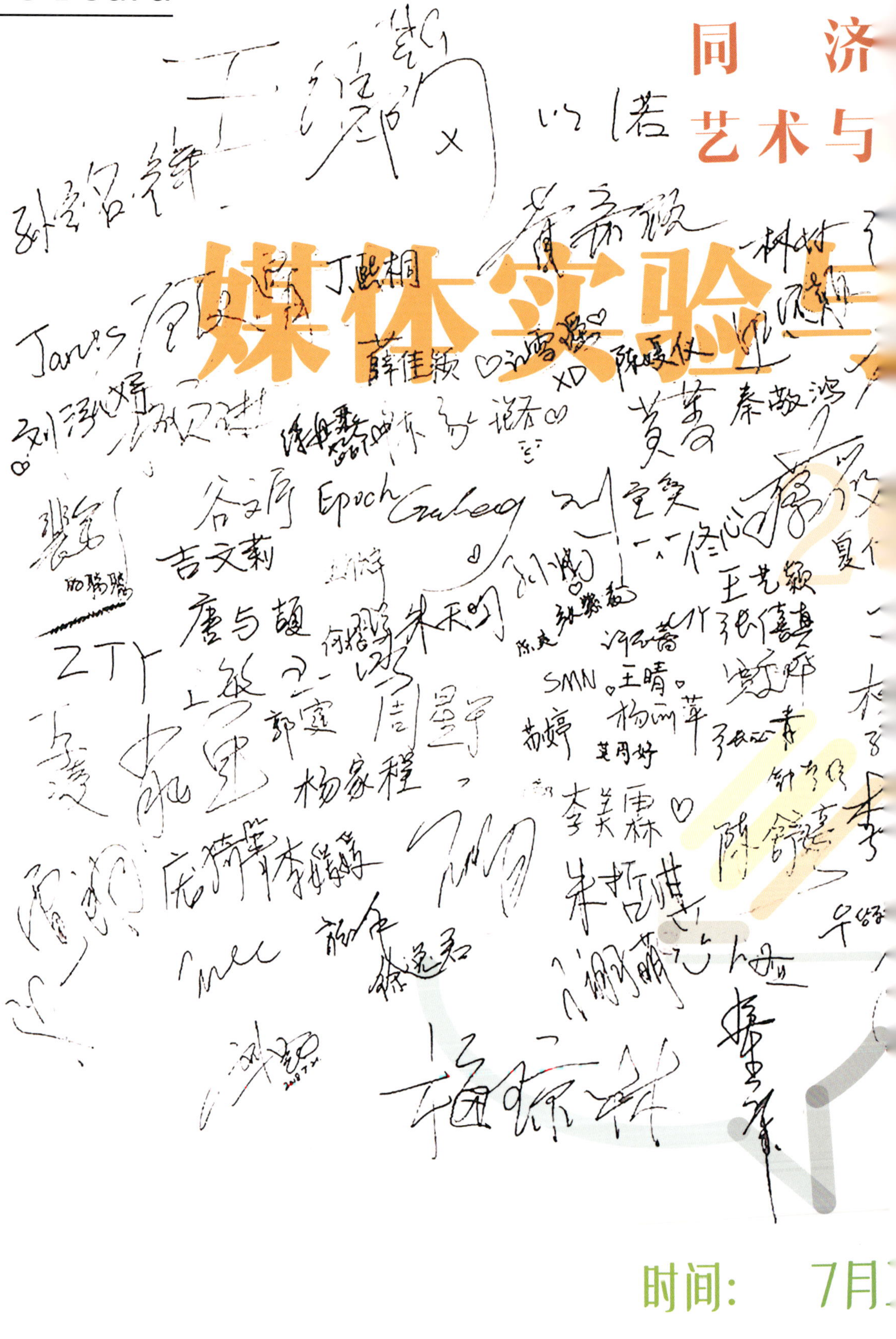

大 学

媒学院

实践工作坊

印名

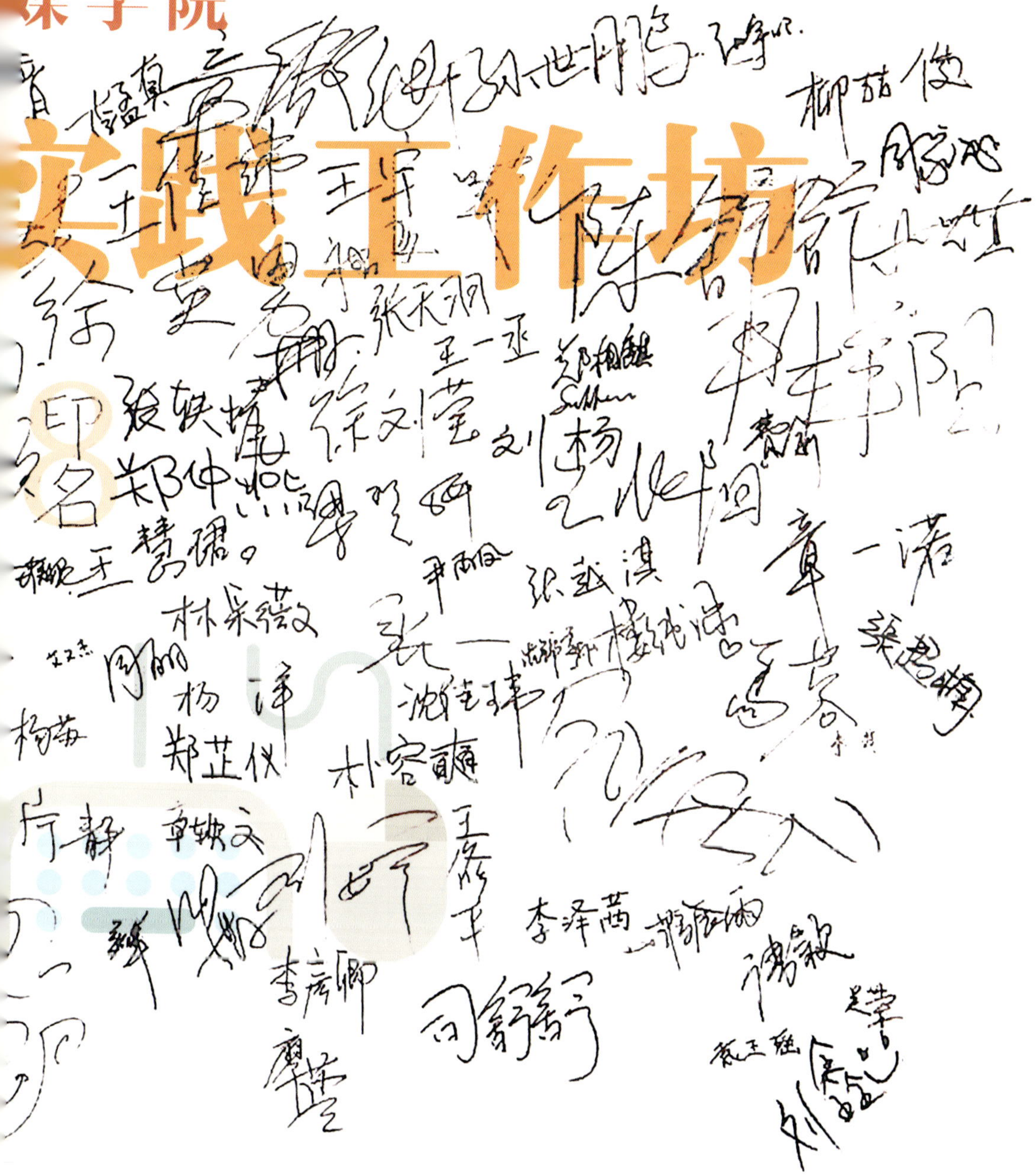

—7月23日

师生大合照

End-of-workshop Photo

福
社会主义 核心 价值观
爱國
敬業
社会主义 核心 价值观
践工作坊
Tongji
1907

融媒体实验与实践工作坊
主　编 / 　金云水　徐逸君
副主编 / 　董　华　刘　芸
文　案 / 　模块课程教师　　徐逸君
翻　译 / 　刘术一　蔡　蕾
摄　影 / 　杨晨青　黄俊仪　杨鉴琳
排　版 / 　徐逸君　许　奕
校　对 / 　金云水　徐逸君
摄　像 / 　王　胜　陈慧玲　丑科钰　鲍雨迪　蒋辰雨

图书在版编目（CIP）数据
融媒体实验与实践工作坊 / 金云水，徐逸君主编
.-- 上海：同济大学出版社，2020.3
ISBN 978-7-5608-8975-7

Ⅰ．①融… Ⅱ．①金…②徐… Ⅲ．①传播媒介－教学研究－高等学校 Ⅳ．①G206.2

中国版本图书馆 CIP 数据核字 (2020) 第 001594 号

出 品 人　华春荣
责任编辑　张　翠　　责任校对　徐春莲
出版发行　同济大学出版社 www.tongjipress.com.cn
地　　址　上海市四平路 1239 号　邮编 200092　电话 021-65985622
经　　销　全国新华书店
印　　刷　上海安枫印务有限公司
开　　本　889mm×1194mm　1/16
印　　张　7
字　　数　224 000
版　　次　2020 年 3 月第 1 版　2021 年 3 月第 2 次印刷
书　　号　ISBN 978-7-5608-8975-7
定　　价　78.00 元